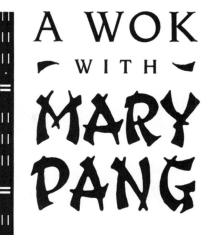

A WOK
~ WITH ~
MARY PANG

Sumi Paintings by:
Reni Moriarity

D1555565

PEANUT BUTTER PUBLISHING
SEATTLE, WASHINGTON

ISBN 0-89716-371-0
Peanut Butter Publishing
200 Second Avenue West
Seattle, Washington 98119

Cover Design: Graphiti Associates
Cover Photographs: Conrad & Company
Food Styling: David Fukukawa Chen
Editor & Book Designer: Nancy M. Pascoe

Table of Contents

Acknowledgments

I would like to acknowledge:
Alyce Hazeltine, the former Home Economics Editor of the Seattle, Wa. morning paper, the *Post Intelligencer*
and
Betty Stout, retired Director of Home Economics of Puget Sound Power and Light Co., Bellevue, Wa.

Many are the fond memories I have of the "Cooking Chinese-Style" appearances Alyce, Betty, and I were in. How did they start? When Alyce introduced me to Betty, and Betty asked if I would be willing to make a speech on Chinese cooking in front of a group of women. I asked "How many?" Betty answered, "About 25 to 35." Sounded simple enough, so I said, "okay." But, that simple speech turned out to be "Cooking Chinese-Style" where I stir-fried a few Chinese dishes in front of an audience of full-capacity crowd of over 200. As Chinese cooking was usually associated with gas, "Cooking Chinese-Style", being done on electric units, was happily welcomed by people using electricity. Consequently, we appeared north, south, east, and west in front of audiences that ranged from 200 to 3000. "Cooking Chinese-Style" was just one venture we were involved in together. There were many other memorable ones, a lot of hard work, but a lot of fun, too.

I will always be grateful to them for devoting so much of their time unselfishly and for adding their presence to give all the events a "celebrity status." And for the many things they taught me. Thanks a million Alyce and Betty for sharing your busy schedules with me.

I would also like to acknowledge:

Bob (Robert) Hardwick, renowned radio announcer, Seattle, Wa., who bravely ate the "100 Year Old Egg" we served him! He has always been willing to lend us a helping hand. Such as being the bartender for a dinner we had donated for charity. And, being the official greeter for a Chinese New Year event, for which he dressed in a black Chinese outfit, black skull cap with black pigtail and a Fu Manchu Mustache and beard, and spoke with a broken English dialect! The guests were first surprised, then thrilled, when they found out who the greeter was.

In spite of his extremely busy schedule, he has always been willing to devote some of it to us when asked, thus giving our events a "celebrity status" with his appearance. Many thanks to you, Bob for the countless number of things you have done for us.

I would also like to acknowledge **Nancy Pascoe**, Editor, who has done an excellent job associating the hints and techniques with the right recipes. Thanks a lot, Nancy, for your patience and cooperation!

And last, but not least, I'd like to acknowledge the many, many others who have been supportive through our ups and downs over the years. It is greatly appreciated. Many thanks to all of you!

I dedicate this book to...

my husband, Harry,
who gave me all these invaluable hints and techniques and some of his well-guarded recipes. Unbeknownst to many, he is always behind the scenes in all my accomplishments. Always ready to encourage me when projects are not proceeding correctly. Always giving unbiased, sound advice when asked. Always patient and understanding. And, always there when I need him.

And, to our son, Martin,
I dedicate this book. If it were not for Martin, this book would never have been assembled and printed. Due to his perseverance and great organizational ability, we are finally rewarded with this book!

And, to my sister, Elsie Huie,
I dedicate this book. She is an excellent cook, constantly sharing her new dishes with me. And, she always believed in us, for which we are very thankful.

And, to our dear grandchildren,
I dedicate this book for their enjoyment when they are old enough to cook.

Meet Mary Pang

There is indeed a Mary Pang behind the well-known red and yellow boxes found in the grocery store. Mary Pang, along with her husband Harry, has been making delicious Chinese frozen foods for about 35 years in a inconspicuous building south of Seattle's China Town/International District. Their son Martin grew up amongst the egg rolls and giant woks to become president of the company. This is a family business dedicated to using the highest quality ingredients to make the tastiest possible Chinese food.

Mary Pang has made innumerable appearances and taught countless classes to show people how to make delicious Chinese food at home. She has demonstrated how to stir-fry vegetables in front of crowds ranging from a dozen to two thousand. Her cooking classes, which are unfortunately no longer offered, were held right in her office next to the frozen foods kitchens. Students still call her to ask when another class is going to begin or with questions about Chinese cooking.

During her appearances and classes Mary discovered what were the most often asked questions and supplied her students with the answers that only a professional Chinese chef would know. These hints and tips, along with her nutritious and easy-to-prepare recipes, are presented in this unique Chinese cookbook.

Chapter One
Getting Started

Getting Started

A Few Hints & Techniques for Getting Started

In these recipes I have used easily obtainable ingredients that can be cooked without special equipment. I have incorporated most of my hints and tips next to the recipe to which they are pertinent. There are a few basic techniques with which you should be familar before you start. There are also a couple of basic kitchen items that you may want to purchase, such as a wok and a Chinese cleaver. But, you do not need to buy these tools. A good, heavy frying pan and a sharp knife are all you need to prepare these delicious recipes.

The Wok

The Chinese wok is the most useful piece of equipment you can have in the kitchen. You can stir-fry in it, boil in it, steam in it, deep-fry in it, use it to make soup, stew, spaghetti sauce and many, many other dishes. There is a round-bottom wok and a flat-bottom wok. The round-bottom wok comes with a metal ring that it sits on. Notice that the metal ring has a large opening on one end and a small opening on the other. When cooking on an electric range set the wok on the large end of the ring, so that the bottom will be closer to the heating unit. When a gas burner is used, set the wok on the small end, as the gas flame can be adjusted up or down to surround the bottom of the wok. The flat-bottom wok sits on the heating unit and is in direct contact with the heat, making it possible to cook over the high heat that is necessary for stir-frying.

Some woks have metal handles on each side, which necessitate using pot holders. Other woks have a metal handle on one side and a long wooden handle on the other. It's simply a matter of personal preference as to which kind of handle you like. Always buy a lid that fits the wok as it is essential for steaming and simmering foods. There are different size woks, but I recommend the 14-inch wok because both large and small portions can be cooked in it.

Some woks come with two cooking tools called "wok-chans." They look like a large deep spoon with a long handle, and a flat spatula with a long handle. They are usually made of steel. If they are not included, buy them separately from an oriental merchandise store. In addition to a pair of long chopsticks, these tools are the best cooking implements you can use when cooking with a wok.

The main feature of a wok is its sloping sides, which are conducive to toss-frying. The wok-chan are used to go down the sloping sides to the bottom, under the vegetables, which are tossed and coated with the hot oil. The reason for tossing the vegetables is to coat all of them with the hot oil which sears in the juices and flavor. This motion is just like tossing a green salad.

Woks are often made of carbon steel and the new ones are sometimes coated with a thin layer of mechanic's grease to protect them against rusting . A new wok should be thoroughly washed with hot, soapy water then rinsed well. Now for seasoning. Place the wok over medium-low heat for a few minutes to open up the pores. Take a paper towel that has been lightly moistened with cooking oil and rub around the inside of the wok. Work the oil into the pores thoroughly. Repeat this heating and oil rubbing process three or four times to season it. After each use, the wok should be washed and dried thoroughly, then put over low heat to slowly finish drying. If the wok is not completely dry it will rust. If your wok does rust, all is not lost. Get a good cleanser and a steel wool pad and briskly scrub away the rust, using lots of elbow grease! If food sticks to the wok the next time you use it, you will need to season it again.

Although the wok is aesthetically pleasing, and a great conversation piece, do not use it as a serving bowl. The food should be removed immediately or it may take on a funny metallic taste.

Electric Woks

There are many types of electric woks available, many of which feature a non-stick surface that do not require seasoning. These are an excellent addition to a kitchen as they can be plugged in anywhere and they come in handy when there is no room on the stove. Follow the manufacturer's instruction for seasoning the wok.

To get the best stir-frying performance from an electric wok keep in mind that the heating unit on these woks is thermostatically controlled, so once the set temperature on the dial is reached, the heating unit turns off. This should not happen during stir-frying because the heat has to be on constantly. If the heat drops your timing will be thrown off and the juices will start exuding from the food. Also the food will stop sizzling — you want to keep it at a sizzle. I usually set the temperature to just under 300° and when it is heated I stir-fry my recipe. If the heating unit goes off while I am stir-frying (the red signal light will turn off when this happens) I turn the heat up just a little to trigger the thermostat mechanism and keep the temperature up. There is a range of up to 450° so you have lots of latitude to finish cooking your meal. An electric wok *with a non-stick surface* makes an excellent serving piece, as you will get no metallic taste.

Please note that there are some brands of electric woks that have a ridge around the circumference of the wok's interior. These are not conducive to toss-frying (or stir-frying; these terms are really interchangeable) because the wok-chan can not make a thorough sweep all the way down to the bottom to toss the vegetables.

The Chinese Cleaver

The Chinese cleaver is made from either carbon steel or stainless steel. The blade is about 3 1/2 by 8 inches and comes in two weights or sizes. They are considered the most versatile and indispensable piece of equipment in a Chinese kitchen. The big cleaver, known as the big knife, is used for chopping meat, splitting poultry, and all the heavy chopping. The other cleaver, which is not as heavy and has a thinner blade, is used for slicing. As with a French knife, you hold the handle with one hand and balance the blade against your curved fingers of the other hand while cutting. Some people, at first, are afraid to use these knives, but after they get the knack won't part with it. Besides slicing with it, you can use the side of the blade for smashing garlic and ginger. The flat part of the wooden handle is good for smashing beans. And it is handy for scoopsing vegetables (with the blade facing away from you) off the cutting board. The Chinese prefer the cleavers made from carbon steel; they think they have a better cutting edge. Carbon steel will rust, but all you need to do is use a nylon scrubbing pad with some cleanser and elbow grease should this happen to your cleaver. The best preventative medicine is to rinse and dry it thoroughly. Each time I use my cleaver, if I am not quite finished preparing a meal, I wipe it clean and set it aside. This is so it won't rust before I get to washing and drying it.

The Stir-fry Technique

Learning the basic stir-fry technique is very important. Stir-frying is what brings out the flavor in all the food that you cook. This is how you do it. Remember, as with learning anything new, you will have to practice, so don't get discouraged.

* Heat the fry pan or wok, then add the oil.

* Once the oil is hot, toss in the salt. It is very important that you add the salt to the hot oil. It gives it a much better flavor. Many people toss the salt over the food after it is cooked. But by adding the salt to the hot oil, the salt can melt in the oil. When the vegetables are added and tossed in the oil, the salt is driven into them, giving them a better flavor and in some cases, preserving their fresh color.

* During one of my appearances, a student asked me why was I pointing a chopstick into the frying pan. This is how I test to see if the oil is hot enough to add the ingredients. Using one dry chopstick, the wooden kind, I press it into the frying pan (or wok), into the oil. If the oil is not hot enough you will not see a sizzle around the chop stick, but if the oil is the right temperature you'll see little bubbles sizzling around the chop stick.

* When the oil is hot, toss in the ingredients in the order called for in the recipe.

* The Chinese utensils, called wok-chans are used to go down the sloping sides to the bottom, under the vegetables, which are tossed and coated with the hot oil. The reason for tossing the vegetables is to coat all of them with the hot oil which sears in the juices and flavor. This motion is just like tossing a green salad.

Stir-fry or Toss-fry

People often ask the difference between stir-frying and toss-frying. Toss-frying is associated with cooking in a wok. Stir-frying is usually associated with stirring the ingredients in a frying pan or pot with straight sides. But regardless, both terms are used interchangeably and are associated with Chinese cooking.

Timing

You will learn to adjust your cooking time depending on how crunchy you like your vegetables. If you like vegetables with some bite then cook them for a shorter amount of time, if you like them a little softer then lengthen their time in the wok. As you cook more and more you will find what you like and what you don't. Adjust to your own taste. It is very important that initially you follow the recipes word for word, however as you become more adept, you should adjust the seasonings and timing to suit your own taste. Not everyone likes things done the same way. It would be an awfully dull world if this were true.

Steaming

The bamboo steamers available at oriental stores are very beautiful but you do not need to purchase one in order to have deliciously steamed Chinese food. To make a steamer at home simply cut both ends off a tuna can, or one pound coffee can, and perforate the sides with a bottle opener. Set the tuna can in a large sauce pan or pot that has a tightly fitting lid. Put in water to about half way up the sides of the can. Use a heat resistant soup plate, or other plate that has sides and put the food that you wish to steam in that. Now simply put the dish on the can, cover the pan and turn the heat on high. You don't want the water to boil too rapidly or have too much water in the pan, as it will splash into the dish and dilute all the delicious juices that are exuding from the food. By perforating the can, the water will boil through it without toppling the whole recipe into the water. Now for the sloping sides of the soup plate; you don't want to lose any of the juices that come from the food while it is cooking! You will be amazed at how much liquid will exude, so be sure you don't make the common mistake of putting the recipe on a flat plate and then watch all of the delicious juices run into the water.

Be careful when you remove the cover from the pan to tilt it away from you. The steam is very hot and can burn.

A Few Basic Ingredients

Cooking Oil

Any kind of tasteless vegetable (or cooking) oil can be used for the stir-fry recipes, it just depends on your personal preference. Many people ask "why do the Chinese use peanut oil?" The reason for using peanut oil is that it has a very high smoking point and it doesn't give off any flavor. Regarding the smoking point, many of you know how quickly butter smokes when it has been placed over high heat, that means it has a low smoking point. You can heat peanut oil to a very high temperature before it starts to smoke, that means it has a high smoking point. In Chinese cooking it is important to use oil that has a high smoking point because it is imperative to stir-fry at a very high temperature. Peanut oil is good, but you can use any type of vegetable oil. I use vegetable oil because it is less expensive, but still has a high smoking point.

Soy Sauce

This seasoning is the most basic, all-purpose and indispensable sauce used in Chinese cooking. The different grades of soy sauce range in terms of color, from a very light brown to almost a blackish-brown color. Soy sauce has a high percentage of sodium, so adjust the salt in your recipe if you are using a large amount.

Garlic

Many of the recipes ask for a clove of fresh garlic, smashed. I prefer to use fresh garlic because you can control the taste and it has a more subtle flavor than the dried garlic powder, which can be overpowering. When I peel a garlic clove I don't actually peel it; I put it on the counter and smash it with the side of a cleaver. In this way the garlic clove opens up and the skin can be easily removed. When peeling garlic I often put it on a board near the edge of a table or the sink, this is so when I hit it with the side of the cleaver my knuckles don't bang into the counter! If you don't have a cleaver, put the garlic in a paper towel and wrap it up, then smash it with a mallet. Smash it just enough to open it. When a recipe calls for minced garlic, smash it harder before mincing, this cuts down on chopping time. Smashing the garlic not only makes it easier to peel, but it also open the cell walls to release the flavor and juice. The smashed garlic is usually browned on both sides in the hot oil before adding the vegetables to be stir-fried. The garlic can be removed before serving, if desired, as some people do not like biting on a piece of garlic.

Ginger
When a recipe calls for a small piece of ginger it should be the size of your thumb, or maybe half the size of your thumb, depending on how well you like the taste of ginger. I like to smash it because, as with garlic, this opens the cell walls and releases the ginger juice to flavor the food. It is important to brown both the ginger and garlic because it imparts a much better taste. I stir-fry it with the other vegetables, then take it out when I serve the dish in case people don't know what it is and eat it by mistake.

Ginger is sold by the pound in the produce section. You don't need to buy the whole piece, simply break off the amount you wish to purchase. Ginger will dry out if left at room temperature. Put it in a plastic bag in the refrigerator or freezer and cut off a piece as needed. I have seen many recipes in other cook books that call for peeled ginger. You do not need to peel ginger because the skin is so thin. At certain times of the year you can get what is called 'young ginger', this is ginger that has not matured. It looks different; it is a little more yellow and the skin is flaky in appearance. This sort of ginger, when sliced thin, is excellent for making Ginger Beef. It has bite but not too much bite. This is the ginger used for making candied ginger and in preserves. The ginger you usually see is older ginger. If this kind of ginger is too hot, you can slice it thinly and blanch it in hot water for a minute of two, depending on how much ginger taste you want.

When a recipe calls for ginger or garlic, try the original recipe first to see how you like the seasoning. Then, the next time you make it, adjust the amount of garlic or ginger to your own personal preference.

If fresh ginger and fresh garlic are not available in your area you can use powdered ginger or garlic, but use it sparingly as it is concentrated. Do not put it in the hot oil — you must add it with the other ingredients as they cook; otherwise, it will burn.

When purchasing powdered garlic, buy the straight garlic powder, not the garlic salt. Garlic salt is a combination of garlic and salt. With the garlic powder you can control the amount of garlic you are using and the amount of salt. Use it sparingly until you find out the amount that suits you.

Tofu

Tofu is a bean cake made from soy beans. It is very nutritious, being high in protein. Tofu is very bland in taste and takes on the flavor of the other ingredients in a dish. There are two types of tofu, the Chinese type, which is firm and the Japanese tofu, which is softer. If the Chinese tofu is not available I buy the Japanese variety and put it in a pan with no water and leave it in the refrigerator. After it sits in the refrigerator a little while water comes out and the tofu becomes firmer. It is very perishable, so keep that in mind when you buy it at the store; be sure to look at the code date. When you take it home, remove the water and put it into a pan of fresh, cold water. If you are not going to use it right away, put it in the refrigerator. Change the water daily. But don't run water directly on the tofu or it will break into pieces. When it starts to go bad it has a slight sour taste.

Toasted Sesame Seeds

Toasted sesame seeds are a popular item used in many of these recipes. I prefer to toast my own. It isn't difficult and the flavor is wonderful. Buy the raw white sesame seeds. They can be purchased in a supermarket or oriental store. Heat a fry pan over medium-low heat, do not put it on too high as sesame seeds scorch very easily. The Chinese toast sesame seeds in a wok, but for home use it is best simply to use a small frying pan — there is no sense in getting out the wok for a few sesame seeds. Do not put oil into the pan, the sesame seeds will exude oil as they toast. Put the seeds in the pan and shake now and then, or stir them around with chopsticks. They must be toasted slowly or they will burn. If you don't have time to stand around and watch them then turn the heat to low so you can look at their progress off and on. When they reach the desired brown remove from the frying pan and place in another container. You will know when they are ready, not only because of the nice brown color, but also because of the toasty fragrance coming from the pan. The sesame seeds, after they have been removed, will still continue to brown a bit. After they cool you should refrigerate them. If you make them ahead of time you may want to retoast them right before using to get back that freshly toasted flavor. Simply shake them again in a pan over medium-low heat until you smell that toasty fragrance. If you leave them in the frying pan you must remember that the pan retains a certain amount of heat and will continue to brown the seeds. Some people toast sesame seeds in an oven but they are not nearly as tasty as the pan-toasted seeds. There is a lot of difference between pan-toasted and oven-toasted. I have been asked by many people why the Chinese sesame seeds are so good — it is because of the pan (or wok) toasting.

Sesame Oil

Have you ever been to a Chinese restaurant and had a bowl of pork noodles, wonton or egg flower soup and wondered what was the delicious seasoning. Often times that taste is toasted sesame oil. You will notice sesame oil being mentioned in many of these recipes. When you buy sesame oil you must get the toasted kind. It is has a burnished look to it. Some people have said to me in my classes that sesame oil is very cheap. If you look in the cooking oil section of your grocery store you may find sesame oil, and it is very reasonably priced compared to the small bottles in the oriental section. However, in these recipes I have used the toasted sesame oil, it is the toasting that gives it the unique taste. The sesame in the other section is not toasted; it is not the one I use. When using sesame oil do not use too much as it is very concentrated. Learn to adjust to your own taste as time goes on. When buying toasted sesame oil look at the label and make sure it is 100% pure. There are some brands on the market that have had the regular cooking oil added to it, therefore cutting the intensity of the oil. The toasted kind of sesame oil should not be used for frying, it is only for seasoning.

Cornstarch

Cornstarch is used very often by the Chinese as a thickener for their sauces. It goes into solution very easily with cold water and is not as heavy in taste as flour. I stressed in my cooking classes the importance of preparation. I like to have everything ready ahead of time, with everything in order so I can get to it easily. But, cornstarch is one thing that can not be prepared in advance. If you mix it ahead of time in water it will settle to the bottom and becomes so hard that it is very difficult to get the corn starch back into solution. The best thing to do is measure out the corn starch into a little dish and set it on the counter, then when you are ready to use it pour in a little water and mix.

Green Onions

To prepare green onions cut off the root and throw that part away. The rest of the onion can be used, green parts and all. Cut the green onion into 1 to 1 1/2 inch lengths. If the white part is thick, cut it in half lenghtwise.

Chinese Tea

Brewing Chinese teas is not like getting a tea bag and some hot water — it is not done that simply. First put very hot water in your tea pot to warm it, meanwhile put cold water in a tea kettle and set it on the stove to boil. The minute the water boils take it off the stove immediately and pour the warming water out of the tea pot and add a tablespoon, or so, of tea leaves. Pour the boiling water in immediately and cover. Then let the tea steep for at least 5 to 10 minutes. You do not drink it immediately like you would a tea bag in a cup of water. Now it is very important that the minute the water boils you take it off the heat immediately. At first Harry, my husband, and I could not figure out why this was so, but there is usually a reason why the Chinese insist on doing things a certain way. We finally figured it out; if you keep boiling the water all the air boils out, consequently the tea has a flat taste instead of a full-bodied taste.

There are various types of tea. One that is popular with the Chinese is chrysanthemum tea. This is actually made with chrysanthemum petals that have been dried. It has a slight bitter taste to it and is generally mixed with a little honey. Another popular tea, rather on the gourmet side, that you don't often see served in a Chinese restaurant, is the jasmine tea. If you look at the tea you will see little white pieces of the jasmine flowers that have been dried; this is what adds the fragrance to the tea. Generally, when the Chinese eat chow mein or fried rice (they consider those dishes to be very rich) they have a special tea, one that is stronger than usual, to drink after the meal to cut the grease and aid digestion. If you have a Chinese store in your area, I suggest you go there and experiment to see what kind of tea you like best.

When you have been at a Chinese restaurant and seen a Chinese host or hostess serve tea at their table, you may have noticed a tapping sound. This sound is made by the guests who are tapping their fingers on the table, "tap tap." They are not practicing the Morse code; they are saying thank you for having tea poured for them. It is impolite to talk with food in your mouth so instead of speaking the words "thank you," the Chinese guest taps. If you should run into a Chinese friend and they say "Nim Cha," which means "drink tea," you will want to say yes. This is an invitation to eat those delicious dishes, served at lunch, dim sum.

And, It's Good for You, too

Chinese cooking, as done in this cookbook, is a very healthy way to eat. Very little oil is used and the vegetables and meats are cooked briefly, so their vitamins and minerals are retained, as well as all their flavor. I recommend using only the freshest available produce, as we do in our frozen foods kitchen.

Chinese cooking is very flexible. Any meat, poultry, or seafood can be substituted for another. If your diet has certain restrictions, delete the item from the recipe and substitute it with something you can eat.

It you are not allowed any oil in your diet, then use the steaming method for cooking in place of the stir-fry technique. Any meat poultry, or seafood can be steamed. Vegetables can be cooked briefly in a good soup stock that has had the grease removed from the surface. The vegetables can be served in the stock or removed from the soup and served alone. Any vegetable cooked briefly will retain its vitamins, minerals, and nutrients whether it's stir-fried or boiled briefly (1 to 2 minutes, depending on the texture and body of the vegetable.)

If salt is restricted from your diet, delete it, soy sauce, and oyster sauce from the recipes.

So with a little imagination in substitution and deletion, follow the cooking techniques and you will not only enjoy your food but eat healthfully.

Chapter Two
Appetizers
& Soups

Appetizers

Wonton

Wontons are those delicious little Chinese dumplings that are made from various fillings wrapped in a pasta-like dough. 'Won' means clouds, 'ton' means swallowing — you are swallowing billowing clouds!

There are various ways of folding the filling into the won ton 'skins' or 'wrappers'. Folding them may take a little practice, but don't get discouraged. Wonton wrappers come packaged by weight. If possible buy the wrappers fresh, as they are easier to handle. If you do buy them frozen, let them defrost naturally in the refrigerator, because if you try to peel them off the stack when they are frozen they will break into little pieces. After wrapping the wontons it is good to lay out them in a row on a paper plate. When you have made a bunch, wrap them and put them in the refrigerator until you are finished with the rest. If you are making a lot, say two to three hours worth of wrapping, it is best to cook some as you go. If you leave them on the plate too long, they tend to stick and when you try to lift them off they will tear and fall apart. If you want to make them ahead, and I always stress preparation, you can freeze them in a strong plastic bag. Pack them in the bag loosely so that you can take out however many you need later. Be sure not to put anything on top of them — when they are frozen, they will crack easily.

Another way to prepare in advance, particularly if you are feeding a large crowd, is to boil the wontons ahead of time. Be sure to add the cold water during the boiling process as per the instructions. This really does keep the won tons whole and perfect. After they are cooked and you have blanched them in a bowl of cold water, sprinkle the water with a couple of tablespoons of cooking oil. Then bring the wontons up through the oiled surface to drain. This will keep the wontons from sticking together. Cover and refrigerate until you are ready to use them. They can be refrigerated for two to three days.

I must caution you, if you do a filling that contains meat and salt or soy sauce, it will retain a pinkish color even after the meat is cooked. Don't worry about the pink. If you have followed the cooking instructions then it really is cooked. The salt or soy sauce partially cures the meat, that is why it retains the pinkish tinge.

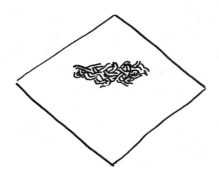

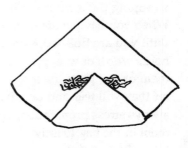

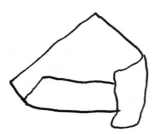

Wonton Meat Filling

1 pound uncooked pork, chopped fine or
coarsely ground
1/4 pound uncooked peeled shrimp,
chopped into small pieces
1/3 cup finely chopped Nappa cabbage
1/2 tablespoon chopped fresh green onions
3 sprigs Chinese parsley, chopped fine
1 egg, beaten
3/4 teaspoon salt
1/2 teaspoon sesame oil
2 teaspoons soy sauce
1/2 tablespoon oyster sauce
1/2 teaspoon sugar
2 teaspoons cornstarch

Mix ingredients together thoroughly.
Refrigerate at least 30 minutes before using.
See illustration on the facing page for how
to wrap.

*Chinese parsley is also known
as cilantro or coriander. It is
used both as a garnish and a
seasoning. Most grocery
stores stock Chinese parsley
year round in their produce
section.*

Three Ways to Cook Wontons

Boiled Wontons

Drop wontons into boiling water, when they float to the surface add 1/2 cup cold water. It is very important to add the cold water or the skins will break apart and all your hard work will be wasted. Let the water boil again and repeat the process once more if the filling is generous. Remove from boiling water, blanch in a pot of cold water to which 1 tablespoon of oil has been added and drain by bringing up through the oiled surface. Set aside until ready to use.

It is very important that the wontons be brought up through the oiled surface — this is what keeps them from sticking together. If you simply pour them into a colander, water and all, the oil will go down the drain, not coat the wontons.

Deep Fried Wontons

Heat 2 inches of oil in a frying pan or wok to 325 degrees. Deep fry both sides of wontons until brown and cooked through. Remove from oil and drain. Serve with sweet and sour sauce, page 173.

These can be made ahead of time and refrigerated in a container that has a tight cover. It must be refrigerated because it has a meat filling. If you are using the wontons with a sweet and sour dip or with foo yee (see page 177), and you want them to be crisp, then put them in a preheated 325° oven until you start smelling the fragrance of the wontons— this means they are ready. Let them cool until ready to use.

Pot Stickers

The pot stickers seen in restaurants have a rather fancy crinkle edge that is difficult to make. I suggest, for home use, that you get the round wonton skins. If you are fortunate enough to have a Chinese noodle factory in your town, see if you can get the round wonton wrappers that are a little bit thicker than normal wonton skins. Depending on your personal preference, put about a teaspoon of filling into the center then fold the wonton wrapper over this to form a half-moon. Dab the edges with water and press firmly to seal.

To prepare ahead of time, brown the pot stickers and refrigerate them until ready to use. Then put them back into the pan and continue cooking as per instructed. Or you can cook them completely then zap them for a minute in the microwave, or reheat them in the pan.

Heat 2 tablespoons oil in a 10" frying pan over medium-high heat, add uncooked wontons. Brown bottoms of wontons, then add 1/2 cup water. Cover frying pan and bring to a boil. Reduce the heat and continue boiling slowly until water evaporates. If the filling is generous, add 1/2 cup more water and continue to cook. Turn the heat down to medium and cook until the bottoms are crispy. Slip a spatula under the pot stickers and flip them over like pancakes onto the serving platter so the brown sides face up. Serve hot. Dip into a sauce made of 1 part vinegar and 1 part soy sauce, or a hot mustard/soy sauce mixture, or hot chili oil.

Drummer Boy Drummettes

Chicken wings — quantity is your choice
Barbecue sauce — enough to cover chicken,
see recipe page 170

Cut off and discard wing tips and save for
soup stock. Disjoint the meaty drummette
from the middle section Cut around the
muscle at the joint to separate the meat from
the bone. Push the meat toward the top of
the drummette to form a small ball.   Place
these drummettes in a shallow glass dish
and brush with barbecue sauce. Refrigerate
and let stand for at least 1 hour, or overnight.

I recommend putting foil on the broiling pan so it won't be so difficult to clean.
Remember to keep the oven door a little bit ajar when you are broiling!

To broil: place drummettes on a foil-covered
broiler pan. Broil 5 to 8 inches from broiler
element, basting occasionally with barbecue
sauce. Cook slowly for 20 to 25 minutes or
until chicken is cooked.

To bake: preheat oven to 500 degrees. Put in
the drummettes and bake for 10 minutes.
Turn heat down to 400 degrees and bake
approximately for 15 more minutes. Turn
and baste drummettes at least once while
cooking.

Serve warm or cold

Hom Bow
Steamed Buns

3 cups warm water
1/4 cup evaporated milk
2 packages active dry yeast
1/4 cup sugar
4 cups flour

You can use your favorite hot yeast roll recipe if you wish. Or, if you need to save time and energy, you can buy the packaged hot roll mix at the grocery.

Combine milk with warm water (temperature should be about 110 degrees). Add dry yeast and sugar, mixing well until the yeast has dissolved. Add about 3 cups of flour until batter is thick and gooey. Cover bowl and let stand for 45 minutes in a warm place, batter will be bubbly. Add the following:

1/3 cup sugar
1 teaspoon salt
5 cups flour (about)

Add enough flour to make a soft dough. Turn dough out onto a lightly floured board, grease hands and knead dough until smooth and elastic. Roll into a ball and place in a greased container with a lid. Let stand in a warm place for about 45 minutes, or until doubled in bulk. Punch down and form the dough into a long long loaf, about 3 inches in diameter. Slice it into 1 1/2 inch pieces. Flatten into rounds, then place 1 tablespoon hom bow meat filling in center. Bring edges together and pinch to seal. Turn upside down onto wax paper that has been placed on a steaming rack. The wax paper prevents the dough from sticking to the rack, but be sure not to eat it! Steam over medium heat for 15 to 18 minutes or until the bow spring back when touched.

These can also be baked in a oven. Brush the tops before removing from the oven with an egg wash made from 1 egg beaten with 1 tablespoon of cold water.

Barbecued Pork Filling for Hom Bow

Learn to have your seasonings in the same spot all of the time, such as having your soy sauce always in the same place in the cupboard.

1 pound barbecued pork, cut into small pieces, see recipe page 146
3 tablespoons green onions, finely chopped
1/2 teaspoon sugar
2 tablespoons hoisen sauce
1/2 cup basic soup stock, see recipe page 169
1 tablespoon soy sauce
Cornstarch mixed with water and soy sauce

Stir-fry barbecue pork, green onions, sugar, and hoisen sauce in a greased frying pan or wok. Add the basic soup stock and thicken with cornstarch mixture. Cool. Makes filling for 16 hom bow.

Butterfly Puffs

1 pound wonton skins
8 ounces crab meat, fresh or canned. If
canned shrimp is used, drain well as they
may be very salty
2 teaspoons finely minced green onions
6 tablespoons mayonnaise
1/4 teaspoon sugar
1/4 teaspoon curry powder
3 ounce package cream cheese, softened
Few drops of sherry wine
Oil for deep frying

Mix cream cheese thoroughly with crab
meat, green onions, mayonnaise, sugar,
curry powder, and sherry. Refrigerate until
ready to use. Place 1/2 teaspoon of this
mixture on wonton skin and wrap around
filling, see page 24. Repeat with the remaining
crab meat filling. Deep fry in oil that has
been heated to 375 degrees. Brown on all
sides, remove from oil, and drain. Serve
hot.

Scallions and green onions are the same thing. The term scallions is used generally back East and in many cookbooks, whereas 'green onions' is used on the West Coast.

Shrimp Egg Rolls

1/3 pound uncooked shrimp, finely chopped
1 1/2 tablespoons oil
1/2 teaspoon salt
1/2 teaspoon sugar
1 cup finely chopped celery
3/4 cup finely chopped onion
1 cup bean sprouts, finely chopped
1/2 cup finely chopped water chestnuts, rinsed and drained
1/4 cup finely chopped bamboo shoots, rinsed and drained
(If mixture is too dry, add cornstarch mixed with water)
12 to 18 egg sheets for wrapping shrimp mixture
Basic batter, see recipe page 168
Oil for deep-frying egg rolls

For the egg sheets:
6 large eggs, approximately
Cooking oil

Making the egg sheets:
You will need a 10" non-stick frying pan. Beat the eggs well and set aside. Put the frying pan over medium-high heat. Oil the frying pan by rubbing a little oil onto it with a paper towel. You need only a slight coating of oil, do not put on too much or the

If you make a mistake when you are cooking Chinese dishes, even if it is for company, do NOT worry about it. As Harry says, "Even monkeys fall out of trees." Your friends, when they are eating your delicious Chinese dishes are so happy to have been invited over that they won't even notice if something is wrong.

egg will not adhere to the pan to form an egg sheet. You will need to oil the pan for each egg sheet, so keep the oiled paper towel handy. When the pan is hot enough, pour some egg batter into the pan and quickly swish it around in a circular motion, then pour the excess egg back into your batter container. You will hear the batter sizzle when it hits the hot pan. The egg sheet is ready to be flipped when it begins to pull away from the sides of the frying pan. Slowing lift it from the pan and flip it onto the other side. Cook on the other side momentarily, just enough to dry it. Pick up the egg sheet and remove it to a plate. Continue with your next sheet. You will probably have to oil the frying pan each time until you master this technique. When you become a master egg sheet-maker you will be able to make two or three without oiling the pan!

This requires a lot of practice. You may want to practice the circular motion of swishing the egg batter into the pan with some water first — just to get the action down before you actually use eggs. The longer you swish the egg batter, the thicker the egg sheet becomes. If the egg sheets are too thick they will crack while cooking and all the ingredients will ooze out. As you get more adept, you will be able to swish quickly and drain off the excess egg to form thinner, more elegant egg sheets. After you have mastered this technique you will practically be able to see through your egg sheets. The trick is to pour off the excess egg right away.

These can be made ahead of time and frozen. But be sure to put them on a paper plate to keep them flat and rigid when they freeze. Do not put anything on top of them in the freezer or they will break into little pieces. When you are ready to use them, remove from the freezer and let thaw at room temperature.

Assembling and cooking the egg rolls:
Heat the oil in a frying pan or wok that has been set over high heat until hot. Add salt then the shrimp and stir-fry until shrimp is pink. Add the sugar, celery, onion, bean sprouts, water chestnuts, and bamboo shoots. Mix thoroughly, cover, and cook until vegetables are tender. Thicken with the cornstarch mixture then cool and chill in refrigerator. Place 1 to 2 tablespoons of the chilled shrimp mixture near the edge of each egg sheet, fold sheet over filling, then roll once. Hang onto roll firmly and tug slightly toward you. This little tug helps get rid of the air so the egg roll doesn't burst open when cooked. Flip sides over filling and continue to roll, then seal with small amount of water mixed with four. Dip egg rolls into the basic batter, then deep-fry in 350 degree oil until golden brown. Drain and serve immediately. Makes 1 to 1 1/2 dozen egg rolls.

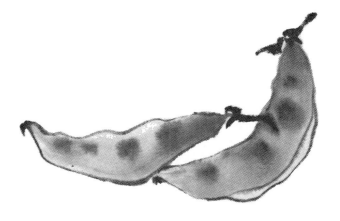

The Soups

Soups

Basic Soup Stock

2 quarts cold water
1 cup sliced, uncooked pork or pork bones, chicken bones, wings, neck, etc.
Salt to taste (approximately 1/2 teaspoon)

Put all of the ingredients into a big pot that has been set over high heat and bring to a boil. Reduce heat to low and simmer gently for 2, or more, hours. Skim scum and fat, strain soup, cool and refrigerate until ready to use. You will be able to lift the solidified fat off the top of your stock. It will keep for about 4 or 5 days.

Any inexpensive cut of meat will do. If you like, you can stock-pile bones from your everyday cooking in the freezer until you have enough to make stock. However, chicken backs are a good deal if you don't have bones handy. Stewing hens, which are no longer as available as they used to be, are quite cheap and have lots of flavor. Do not throw the skin away, it contains much flavor.

If you are planning a dinner for later in the week, you can make the stock ahead and refrigerate it for 4 to 5 days.

Stock freezes well. I like to freeze it in ice cube trays then pop the frozen cubes into a bag in the freezer. In this way I can defrost a little, or a lot, as needed. If you want you can slowly simmer the stock and concentrate it, that way you don't have as much to store in the freezer.

Spinach Soup

Iceberg lettuce is a delicious substitution for the spinach in this recipe.

If you want to make soup and you don't have any homemade soup stock on hand this is what you can do. Buy the canned clear chicken broth from your grocery store. (Examine the ingredients label to find one without MSG.) It is good to have on hand in a pinch. It may have too strong a chicken taste, in which case add 1/4 can of water to it and bring it up to a boil. If you want a fuller flavored soup, add a few slices of uncooked pork and boil it for about 3 or 4 minutes until the meat is cooked. Or for more chicken flavor, add some sliced raw chicken to the canned stock and boil for 3 minutes. Left over meat can also be thrown into the stock and heated to get rid of the refrigerated taste and kill any bacteria.

4 cups basic soup stock, see recipe page 39
1 bunch fresh spinach (more if desired) washed, stems removed, and each leaf torn into 2 or 3 pieces
Salt to taste
1 teaspoon sesame oil

Bring the soup stock, spinach and salt to a boil and continue boiling for approximately 1/2 to 1 minute, depending on the texture of the spinach. Do not cover the pot as it will over-cook the spinach! Add the sesame oil to the soup, stir, and remove from heat immediately. Serve right away. Makes 4 servings.

Egg Flower Soup with Peas, Mushrooms, and Water Chestnuts

4 cups basic soup stock, see recipe page 39
1 egg, beaten
1 1/2 tablespoons cornstarch, mixed with 1
1/2 tablespoons cold water
1/2 cup fresh or frozen peas (thawed)
1/2 cup sliced, water chestnuts
1/2 cup sliced mushrooms
1 green onion, cut into pieces
1 teaspoon sesame oil
Salt to taste

Bring the basic soup stock to a boil. While soup is boiling slowly pour in the beaten egg, stirring soup vigorously at all times. Next, slowly stir in cornstarch mixture. Then add the peas, sliced water chestnuts, and sliced mushrooms to soup. Bring soup to a boil again, and immediately remove from heat. Add green onion and sesame oil to soup. Stir, then serve. Makes 4 servings.

'Egg flower soup' is known by that name on the West Coast, but on the East Coast it is called 'egg drop soup.'

When beating in the eggs be sure the stock is at a rolling boil, so that the instant the eggs drop in they cook.

Wonton Soup

If you don't already know how to parboil, it is very simple. Put the bok choy into a pot of boiling water, bring it back to a boil, then set your timer for 1 minute. Drain, then stop the cooking action by running cold water over the bok choy.

Never leave the wontons in the soup for several hours or overnight as the broth will seep all the the flavor from the wontons.

4 cups basic soup stock, see recipe page 39
Salt to taste
32 boiled wontons, see recipe page 26
2 teaspoons soy sauce
Few drops sesame oil
1 green onions, sliced
3/4 cup bok choy, parboiled
3/4 cup cooked sliced chicken, barbecued pork, or ham

Heat the basic soup stock and add salt to taste. Put boiled wontons, (8 per person, or more if you want) into boiling soup stock and continue to simmer until wontons are hot, about 1/2 minute. Put 1/2 teaspoon of soy sauce and a few drops of sesame oil into the bottom of 4 individual soup bowls. Then place the wontons into each bowl, topping with green onions, a few pieces of the bok choy, and a few slices of meat or chicken. Pour hot soup over wontons. Makes 4 servings.

A Wok with Mary Pang

Yee Foo Wonton
Fried Wonton in Thick Soup

4 cups basic soup stock, see recipe page 39
24 fried wontons, see recipe page 27
1/3 cup diced water chestnuts, rinsed and drained
1/3 cup diced bamboo shoots, rinsed and drained
1/3 cup diced uncooked chicken meat
1/4 cup fresh or frozen peas
1 teaspoon sesame oil
2 tablespoons cornstarch, mixed with a little water
Few pieces of tomato for color
green onions, sliced for garnish
Salt to taste

Bring the soup stock to a boil. Add the water chestnuts, bamboo shoots, chicken meat, and salt and continue to boil for 3 minutes. Thicken soup with the cornstarch mixture until it becomes the consistency of a thin gravy. Add the peas and sesame oil, and boil 1/2 minute longer before adding the tomato pieces. Place the fried wontons (6 per person) in a large bowl. Pour hot soup over wontons, and garnish with the fresh green onions. Makes 4 servings.

This soup is very popular in San Francisco. Every time Harry and I go to San Francisco we have to eat yee foo wonton at least once.

The fried wontons add an entirely different taste from the regular ones.

Nappa Soup

Nappa cabbage
It is one vegetable you do not have to worry about over-cooking. The longer nappa cabbage cooks the sweeter it becomes. Ginger is often used with nappa because it comple-ments it.

Dried small shrimp
You will see these in a Chinese store. They come in all different sizes, the small ones are less expensive and are the ones to use in the soup. Throwing a little bit in it adds a lot of flavor. It should be put in at the very beginning so it can soften and impart all the delicious flavor.

4 cups basic soup stock, see recipe page 39
1 pound nappa cabbage, cut into chunks
1 egg
Few drops sesame oil
1 small piece fresh ginger, smashed
1 tablespoon dried small shrimp

Combine fresh ginger and dried shrimp with soup stock and bring to a boil. Turn down heat and simmer slowly for at least 20 minutes. After which time bring soup stock back to a rolling boil, add nappa cabbage and continue to boil for 2 minutes, or longer if desired. Add sesame oil, then pour soup into a large serving bowl. Break raw egg into the soup (it will poach in the hot liquid) and serve. Makes 4 to 5 servings.

Watercress Soup

4 cup basic soup stock, see recipe page 39
2 bunches watercress (1 if the bunches are particularly large), washed thoroughly and cut into 3" - 4" lengths, if long
1/2 cup sliced chicken, uncooked
Salt to taste
Few drops of sesame oil, optional

Bring basic stock to a boil and add salt. Next add the chicken and cook for 2 minutes. Add watercress and cook another minute. Put in a few drops of sesame oil if you wish. Serve immediately. Serves 4.

Watercress, a small green, leafy, tender-stemmed vegetable, is sold in small bunches in the produce section of most grocery stores. It is widely used as a garnish or in a green salad. Watercress when eaten raw has a slightly hot bite to it. But, it is delicious and has an entirely different taste when stir-fried or cooked in soup stock.

All About Winter Melon

Winter melon resembles a watermelon, but its surface is not as smooth as a watermelon's; it has ridges and dips and a powdery covering. It is called winter melon because it is plentiful in the winter time. Although it is called winter 'melon' it is actually a squash. You will see them at the grocery or, more commonly, in a Chinese store. They are cut into portions, wrapped in plastic and sold by the pound. Sometimes you can buy them whole, but that is generally too much melon for home use. Choose a piece that is thick-meated, white and firm. Feel it, and if it seems soft, do not buy it.

A favorite banquet treat is winter melon soup that has been cooked right in the winter melon itself. The top is cut off and the seeds and fibers are hollowed out. Then the soup ingredients are put in and the top is replaced. The winter melon is next put into a steamer where it is steamed for hours. When it is removed you can serve directly from the melon by ladling some soup and then scooping out a portion of winter melon from the sides into each bowl. This is quite a showstopper.

Dong-Gwa Dow-Foo Tong
Winter Melon and Tofu Soup

6 cups basic soup stock, see recipe page 39
6 canned water chestnuts, diced, rinsed, and
drained
1 tofu cake, diced
Salt to taste
1/2 pound winter melon, skin removed, and
diced
1/2 cup diced button mushrooms
1/2 cup diced chicken, uncooked
1 teaspoon soy sauce
1 teaspoon sesame oil
Fresh green onions, sliced

Bring the soup stock to a boil in soup pot or
wok and add water chestnuts, winter melon,
mushrooms, chicken, salt, and soy sauce.
Boil this gently for 4 minutes before adding
tofu and sesame oil. Continue to boil for 1
minute. Winter melon becomes translucent
when it is cooked. Sprinkle cut green onions
on top as garnish and serve from a large
soup bowl. Makes 6 to 8 servings.

*Kohlrabi can be used in place
of winter melon in this recipe.
Peel it and cut it into slices or
chunks*

*Jicama is a large root vegetable
that is very interesting and
available in the produce section
of many stores. When peeled
and sliced it tastes like water
chestnut and has the same
crispness. It is good raw and
stir-fried. Stir-fry it only long
enough to heat it through, or it
will lose its crispness. It is
interesting to add jicama to
soup at the very end of the
cooking time — it adds a nice
sweetness and crispness.*

Chapter Three
Rice, Noodles
and Vegetables

Rice

All About Rice

You can go to the same store, to the same shelf, buy the same rice each time, yet it seems to cook differently. We cook rice by the hundreds and hundreds of pounds in our frozen food kitchen and every time we get a new lot, Harry tests the first sack to see what it is like. If it is too soft Harry cuts down on the water a little, if too dry a little more water is added. This is the same supplier, same variety of rice from the same state, but each time it comes in we still have to test it. The rice comes from different farmers and different fields. In addition, rice is like potatoes; there are new potatoes and old potatoes. When the potatoes are new you need less water to cook them; when the are older you need more. Rice is the same. When rice is first harvested it contains more water so less water is needed for cooking; when it is older some of the moisture has evaporated so you need a little more water to cook it. That is another reason why, even though you get the same type of rice each time, the amount of water needed to cook it properly will vary.

In selecting rice it is very important to buy the right kind of rice. I know it is very confusing, there are so many different types, but you need to buy the long grain rice. This is the kind of rice, as a rule, the Chinese use. Many times people have followed the instructions I have given them and they will come back to me and say that the rice was sticky. So I ask them what kind of rice they used, and invariable they had cooked the California pearl rice, which is shorter and stubbier. That variety of rice is sticky, no matter how you cook it. Long grain rice, however, if cooked properly, is not sticky. There is a variety of long grain rice that comes from California; this rice at times can be sticky. The Chinese prefer the long grain rice grown in Texas. It taste better and is drier.

Wash the rice in a bowl of cold water by rubbing it between your hands gently or by swishing it around in a circular motion, then drain. Do this two or three times. The directions on rice packages tell you not to wash the rice. It is believed that when the rice is washed all the nutrients are washed out. Don't worry about the vitamins you are supposedly washing away. If you cook your vegetables properly you will be getting more than your share of vitamins every day. Again, wash the rice. If you had seen the hundreds of pounds of rice that we have cooked in our frozen food kitchen I am sure that you would wash every pound of rice you buy. I swear, when we wash the rice it sometimes looks as though it had been swept up off the floor! Also, when you wash the rice you will notice how milky the water appears. The washing water contains some of the starch that adheres to the grains and contributes to making the rice sticky.

When you measure the water according to the recipe, you measure to the first joint of your index finger, approximately 1 to 1 1/4 inches with the tip of your finger just touching the top of the rice. Do not stick your finger to the bottom of the pot; measure just the water. I had a student once who said she followed the directions but her rice was still mushy. I asked how she measured and she showed me her finger. Well, when I looked at her finger I noticed she had *very* long fingernails, and apparently she had measured her water from the tip of her fingernail! This added a good 1/4 inch of water.

The Automatic Rice Cooker
I personally don't use an automatic (or electric) rice cooker but I am told that they are a boon for busy people. Many rice cookers have a warm setting that allows you to cook the rice and keep it warm for whenever you want it. The Chinese have a reputation of being excellent rice-cookers. I got the surprise of my life one time when I asked one of the Chinese women who work for me to watch a large pot of rice while I fixed lunch. I told her to turn down the heat after it had boiled enough. Well, she looked at me and asked, "When do I turn it down, how will I know?" I said to do it the same way she does it at home. But she said, "I don't cook rice this way, I use an automatic rice cooker." I couldn't believe it!

Boiled Rice

2 cups of long grain rice
Enough cold water to measure to the first joint of the index finger (approximately 1 to 1 1/2 inches)

Wash the rice as explained in *All About Rice*. Place drained rice in a 2 quart sauce pan, add cold water, and cover pan with lid. Bring to a boil over high heat, then reduce the heat to medium and continue to boil until the water has been absorbed, (approximately 10 minutes). Turn heat to low and continue to cook for about 15 minutes longer. Fluff rice gently with a fork or chopsticks. Cover and set aside for 2 to 5 minutes. Makes 4 to 6 servings.

The cover should be left on at all times, except of course when it is time to check if the water has been absorbed. The cover concentrates the heat and cooks the rice. Do not turn the rice down to low immediately after the water has started to boil, even though many instructions tell you to do so. You want to keep the temperature high so that the steam will push up through all the rice. In this way you avoid having sticky rice at the bottom of the pan and rice that is barely cooked at the top. You may put the cover on slightly ajar if the pan is a bit too small and the rice and water are boiling over, but as soon as the boiling subsides, cover the pot immediately.

Fried Rice with Ham

Some people think that the only time you can cook fried rice is when you have day old rice. This is not true! If you want fried rice today then make a pot of fresh rice and continue cooking from there. It isn't that day old rice is best, making fried rice from left-over rice is simply a way of not wasting food.

Scrambling the eggs and setting aside in a bowl until ready to use is a crucial technique. If you pour the uncooked egg in with the rice and mix it you will not be able to see the egg; it will be stuck on the grains of rice.

4 cups cooked long grain rice
2 eggs, beaten
1/2 cup diced ham
4 tablespoons cooking oil
1 tablespoon oyster sauce
3 tablespoons soy sauce
1 green onion, cut into pieces
1 leaf lettuce, shredded
Salt to taste

Heat 1 tablespoon of the oil in a frying pan or wok and add salt, stir. Scramble the eggs, break them apart into small pieces, and set aside in a bowl. Heat the remaining 3 tablespoons of oil in the pan, add the meat, and stir-fry for about 1 minute. Add the cooked rice and mix well, then add soy sauce and oyster sauce, stirring thoroughly. Stir-fry mixture until hot. Add cut green onions, shredded lettuce, and scrambled eggs to the rice mixture. Heat for 1 minute. Makes 4 to 6 servings.

Fried Rice with Chicken

4 cups cold cooked long grain rice
2 eggs, beaten
1/2 cup diced chicken meat, uncooked
4 tablespoons cooking oil
3 tablespoons soy sauce
1 tablespoon oyster sauce
1 green onion, cut into pieces
1 leaf lettuce, shredded
Salt to taste

Heat 1 tablespoon of the oil in a frying pan or wok. Add salt to the oil and scramble the eggs, set aside in a bowl, and break the eggs into small pieces. Heat the remaining 3 tablespoons of oil in the pan and add the meat, stir-fry for about 2 minutes. Then add cooked rice and mix well. Add soy sauce and oyster sauce, and mix thoroughly. Stir-fry this mixture until hot. Add cut green onions, shredded lettuce, and scramble eggs to rice. Heat for about 1 minute and serve. Makes 4 to 6 servings.

Adding the cut green onions right before you finish stir-frying will allow the onions to release their flavor into the rice.

Adding the lettuce with the rice allows the lettuce to take on some to the flavors of the fried rice and gives the dish a refreshing crunchiness.

Fried Rice with Shrimp

Do not use canned shrimp for this recipe. They smell funny and many brands are salty.

4 cups cold cooked long grain rice
2 eggs, beaten
1/2 cup cooked, small shrimp meat, preferably fresh-frozen
4 tablespoons cooking oil
1 tablespoon oyster sauce
3 tablespoons soy sauce
1 green onion, cut into pieces
1 leaf lettuce, shredded
Salt to taste

Heat 1 tablespoon of the oil in a frying pan or wok. Add salt to the oil and scramble eggs, set aside in a bowl, and break eggs into small pieces. Heat the remaining 3 tablespoons oil in the wok and add shrimp, stir-fry for about 1 minute. Next add cooked rice and mix well. Then add soy sauce and oyster sauce, and mix thoroughly. Stir-fry rice mixture until hot. Add cut green onions and scramble eggs to rice, heat for 1 minute. Serve on a platter surrounded by shredded lettuce. Makes 4 to 6 servings.

Mastering the stir-fry technique is very important. When Harry and I go to a restaurant we can tell if the dish has been prepared by the dishwasher cook or the head chef.

A Wok with Mary Pang

Noodles

Stir-fried Noodles with Ginger

5 ounces Chinese egg noodles, the dried
variety
4 tablespoons oil
1/2 teaspoon salt
1 clove garlic, smashed & peeled
1 tablespoon thinly sliced fresh ginger, cut
into very thin strips
4 green onions, cut into 1 1/2" lengths
1 teaspoon sesame oil
2 to 3 tablespoon oyster sauce
1/4 teaspoon sugar

Bring to a boil 1 quart of water, add noodles.
Cook as per direction on package or until al
dente (approximately 4 minutes). Remove
pot from the heat, pour 1 tablespoon of oil
over the surface and stir. With a wire,
bamboo-handled strainer bring noodles up
through the oiled surface. Drain thoroughly.

Heat a frying pan or wok over high heat.
Add the remaining 3 tablespoons of oil, heat
until very hot. Add salt and stir, then add
garlic and brown. Add ginger and green
onions, and stir-fry for about 1 minute.
Next put the noodles into the wok and stir-
fry until hot. Remember to keep the temperature high. Add the sesame oil, oyster
sauce, and sugar; mix thoroughly. Serve immediately.

Noodles
*In browsing around a Chinese
store, you will see many types
of noodles, thick ones, thin
ones, etc. You will see egg
noodles made from wheat flour;
transparent, very thin vermicelli called bean thread noodles
that are made from mung
beans and are high in protein;
and rice sticks, made from rice
flour.*

*It is very important to bring
the noodles up through the
oiled surface. This technique
keeps the noodles separate.*

Curry Beef Lo Mein

"Lo' means mix and 'mein' means noodles.

If you have a Chinese store in your area, buy the curry powder there and ask which brand is popular with their Chinese customers. Some currys are very hot, so adjust to your own taste.

1 pound fresh Chinese egg noodles, or 12 ounces dried
1 pound flank steak, sliced 1/4" thick across the grain
1 tablespoon soy sauce
2 teaspoons sherry wine (optional)
1 clove garlic, minced
1/4 teaspoon sugar
1/4 teaspoon salt, or as desired
1 1/2 tablespoons oil
2 tablespoons cornstarch
1/2 teaspoon salt, or as desired
1 clove garlic, smashed and peeled
1/2 pound sugar peas, tips and strings removed, washed, and drained
1 medium onion, cut into small wedges
1/4 teaspoon sugar
5 tablespoons curry powder
5 tablespoons oil
1/2 cup soup stock, see recipe page 169
1/2 tablespoon cornstarch mixed with 1/2 tablespoon cold water
4 green onions, cut into 2" lengths

Bring to a boil 1 quart of water, add noodles. Cook as per directions on package, or until al dente (approximately 4 minutes). Remove pot from the heat, pour 1 tablespoon oil over the surface and stir. With a wire bamboo-handled strainer bring noodles up through the oiled water. Drain thoroughly. Mix the soy sauce, sherry wine, minced garlic, salt, and sugar together to make a marinade and add the flank steak. Then add the 1 1/2 tablespoons oil, mix. Next add the 2 tablespoons of cornstarch. Set aside.

Heat a frying pan or wok over high heat. Add 2 tablespoons of the oil and heat until hot. Add marinated beef, spreading it evenly over the hot surface. Fry for 1/2 minute, then stir briskly for another 1/2 minute. Remove immediately to a separate dish. Add another 2 tablespoons of the oil to the wok that has been set over high heat. Add salt and garlic; brown the garlic. Then add sugar peas, onion, and sugar. Stir-fry for about 1 minute. Swish 1/2 tablespoon water into the wok. This will remove some of the crust and drippings left on from by cooking the beef and the flavor will cling onto the vegetables while they are stir-fried. After adding water stir-fry for a few more seconds then remove to a dish. Add remaining oil to the wok that has been set over high heat. When the oil is hot, remove from the heat, add curry powder (it should sizzle) and mix. Return to the heat and continue mixing for a few more seconds until you smell the fragrance of curry, then immediately add the 1/2 cup of soup stock, and when it is boiling, slowly stir in the cornstarch mixture. When thickened, add noodles and toss until hot. Add cooked meat, vegetables, and green onions. Stir briskly. Serve immediately.

The curry is stir-fried to remove the "green" taste and to impart a more fragrant curry smell and flavor.

It is nice to save out a few pieces of cooked sugar peas, meat and green onions to garnish the top of the noodles.

Pork and Shrimp Lo Mein

Fresh noodles are those that have not been dried. They are usually sold in one or two pound packages and are in the refrigerated section. The dried Chinese noodles are sold in packages found in the grocery store shelf, often times in the Oriental section. If the fresh noodles are not available then use the dried variety. Chinese noodles have a smoother and more elastic texture than, say Italian pasta. Fresh noodles require less cooking time than the dried ones, approximately 2 to 3 minutes. For the dried noodles follow the cooking time on the package.

1 pound fresh egg noodles, or 12 ounces dried noodles
4 tablespoon oil
1/2 pound small shrimp, preferably fresh-frozen
1/4 pound cut sliced pork
1/2 cup sliced celery
1 onion, cut into slices
1 tablespoon sherry wine
2 tablespoon soy sauce
salt to taste

Bring to a boil 1 quart of water, add noodles. Cook as per direction on package or until al dente (approximately 4 minutes). Remove pot from the heat; add 3 cups cold water then drain immediately. Put the noodles in a bowl of cold water, pour 1 tablespoon oil over the surface and stir. With a wire, bamboo-handled strainer bring noodles up through the oiled water. Drain thoroughly.

Heat oil in wok or frying pan over high heat, add salt and stir. Add pork and stir-fry for 2 to 3 minutes. Next stir-fry the onions and celery for 1 minute. Add shrimp and stir-fry for another minute. Swish sherry down and around the hot sides of the wok so it sizzles. Add noodles and soy sauce and stir-fry until hot. Serve immediately. Makes 5 to 6 servings.

A Wok with Mary Pang

Pork Chow Mein

4 cups fresh or dried Chinese noodles, parboiled and pan-fried, see recipe next page or page 65 for oven method
1 1/2 tablespoons oil
1 teaspoon salt, or to taste
1 clove garlic, smashed
1 cup diced or sliced uncooked pork
1 teaspoon soy sauce
1 teaspoon sesame oil
2 tablespoons oyster sauce
1/2 cup sliced water chestnuts, rinsed and drained
1/2 cup sliced bamboo shoots, rinsed and drained
1 cup bean sprouts
1 cup sliced celery
1 cup sliced Chinese vegetables (bok choy, nappa cabbage, sugar peas, or other vegetables in season)
1 teaspoon sugar
1 1/2 cups basic soup stock, see recipe page 169
1 1/2 tablespoon cornstarch mixed with water

Chow Mein/Chop Sui
Many people have asked me what the difference is between chow mein and chop sui. They look so much alike. 'Chop' means cut and 'sui' means small, so it is cut small. You will notice that the vegetables are all cut into bite-sized pieces. 'Chow' means fried or stir-fried and 'mein' means noodle, this is a stir-fried noodle dish. Once you add fried noodles to the chop sui it becomes chow mein.

To pan-fry noodles:
4 cups cooked noodles
7 tablespoons oil

Heat a wok or frying pan over high heat.
Add 2 of the tablespoons of oil to the pan.
Add noodles and mix over high heat.
Spread the noodles evenly in the pan, to the
edges. Swirl 3 more tablespoons of oil
slowly around the rim of the frying pan just
above the noodles. Cook over medium heat
until the noodles are browned on one side
and no longer stick to the bottom. Flip them
over to the other side like a pancake. Swirl 2
more tablespoons of oil slowly around the
rim of the frying pan, again just above the
noodles. Cook over medium heat until the
noodles are browned. Remove to a serving
platter and put into a 200° preheated oven,
with the door slightly ajar, to keep warm.
Put 1 1/2 tablespoon of the oil in a wok or
frying pan and set over high heat. When the
oil is hot add the 1/2 teaspoon salt and the
garlic, brown garlic slightly, then add the
pork, and stir-fry for 2 minutes. Add soy
sauce, sesame oil, oyster sauce, and mix.
Add all the vegetables, the sugar, the
remaining 1/2 teaspoon of salt, and mix
thoroughly. Cook for about 2 minutes before
adding soup stock. Bring mixture to a boil
and thicken with cornstarch to desired consistency. Add pan-fried noodles and mix.
Makes 4 to 6 servings.

*Quite often the Chinese like to
sprinkle a little vinegar on
their chow mein. There is a
Chinese vinegar that can be
purchased at Chinese grocers,
however, the malt vinegar is
similar and you can buy it in a
regular store. The reason for
using vinegar is to cut the
grease and aid digestion.*

Oven-Browned Noodles:

An excellent and easy way to brown noodles, particularly if you are expecting a crowd, is to put them under the broiler in the oven. Drain the 4 cups of noodles and mix them with 1 1/2 tablespoons oil, 1 table- spoon soy sauce, 1 teaspoon sesame oil, and 2 tablespoon oyster sauce. Mix it well and spread them in a shallow pan. Put the pan in the oven, as close as possible to the broiling unit, and leave the door slightly ajar. When the noodles get nice and brown, mix them around so the rest can brown. When all of the noodles have reached the desired color, turn off the broiler and move the pan lower in the oven to wait. In the meantime, while the noodles are browning, you can stir-fry the vegetables, etc. Then when the noodles are ready you can add them to the wok or frying pan and toss.

This is a good technique for serving a large group because you can brown so many more noodles at one time in a pan in the broiler than in a wok or frying pan. You can really only cook enough noodles in a wok for about 4 people. Also, you can be using your wok to stir-fry the vegetables while the noodles are browning. This method is also less greasy than the pan-fried technique.

Wor Mein
A Glorified Pork Noodle

4 cups cooked noodles
6 cups basic soup stock, see recipe page169
1 cup sliced cooked meat (chicken, barbecued pork, ham, shrimp, squid, chicken giblets, etc.)
1/2 cup sliced bamboo shoots, rinsed and drained
1/2 cup sliced water chestnuts, rinsed and drained
1/2 cup sliced mushrooms
1 cup Chinese greens, sliced and parboiled
2 teaspoons sesame oil
2 tablespoons soy sauce
1 green onion, cut into 1/2" lengths
Hard cooked eggs, sliced for garnish

If you want to have all the meat and other ingredients displayed on top of the noodles, first heat the noodles until they are hot and put them in your serving bowl. Next add the meats, bamboo shoots, water chestnuts, Chinese greens, and mushrooms to the soup stock in the pot. When they are hot, pour everything over the noodles. Add soy sauce and sesame oil. Garnish with egg slices and green onions. Serve hot.

Put the soup stock into a large pot and bring to a boil. Add noodles, soy sauce, meats, bamboo shoots, water chestnuts, and mushrooms. Bring slowly back to a boil. Pour the soup into large serving bowl and add sesame oil and Chinese greens. Garnish with the green onions and egg slices. Makes 4 to 6 servings.

A Wok with Mary Pang

Barbecued Pork Noodles

8 ounces dried Chinese noodles, cooked and drained
4 cups basic soup stock, see recipe page 169
1/2 pound bok choy, cut diagonally in 1 inch pieces and parboiled
1 1/2 hard boiled eggs, cut into halves
3 stalks green onions cut into 1/4 inch pieces
1/2 pound sliced barbecued pork
3 teaspoons soy sauce
1 1/2 teaspoons sesame seed oil

Use 3 large, individual soup bowls. In the bottom of each bowl put about 1 teaspoon of soy sauce, 1/2 teaspoon sesame oil, and as much cut green onion as you like. Heat the soup stock and have other ingredients handy. Pour a little of the hot soup stock into each bowl and mix. Add the hot noodles. Pour remaining soup over noodles. Arrange 1/2 hard boiled egg in center of bowl. At random, place sliced bar-becued pork and pieces of each parboiled bok choy. If desired, sprinkle some more cut green onion on top for garnish. Serve hot. Serves 3.

This is about enough for 3 bowls of noodles. If more noodles are desired, cook more!

To parboil boy choy, throw bok choy into boiling water and boil for approximately 1 minute. Drain and set aside until ready to use.

If desired, other types of meat, poultry, or seafood can be added, as well as other vege-tables, such as parboiled nappa, sugar peas, etc.

To stretch your barbecued pork and make it look like a lot, pile a few slices together then cut into strips and sprinkle over the top of the noodles.

In place of hard-boiled eggs use egg strips. Refer to recipe for making egg sheets, page 34. Cut egg sheets in half. Pile one on top of the other and cut into strips. Cover tightly with plastic wrap and refrigerate until ready to use, as they dry out easily. Loosen egg strips and sprinkle at random over the tops of the noodles.

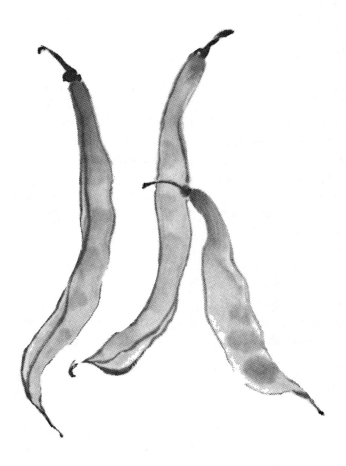

A Wok with Mary Pang

Vegetables

All About Spinach

Select spinach that is green and firm, not yellow and withered. There are certain times of the year when young spinach is available. When spinach is young it has nice smooth green leaves, whereas older spinach has ruffled leaves and the stems are difficult to break off. If the spinach is older, cook it just a little longer than the recommended cooking time.

Spinach is another one of those vegetables to which children often say "ugh!". But if you stir-fry spinach with bacon, many of the "ugh"-sayers will like it, not only because of the bacon flavor, but also because you are not cooking the spinach to death.

Spinach and lettuce are both leafy vegetables and take about the same amount of time to cook. But when you cook cabbage, although it is leafy, it is thicker and harder. The cooking time and the additional water requirement, if any, is similar to broccoli. Other vegetables that are similar to broccoli are string beans, asparagus, cauliflower, celery and any others that have a lot of body. After stir-frying broccoli and spinach a few times you should be able to stir-fry any vegetable you see in the produce section.

A Wok with Mary Pang

Spinach Cooked Chinese-Style

1 pound fresh spinach (washed, stems removed, cut, or torn into small pieces, drained thoroughly)
1 small clove garlic, smashed
2 tablespoons oil
Salt to taste

Pour oil in a frying pan or wok and heat over high heat until very hot. Add salt and garlic, and stir until garlic is brown. Add spinach and mix thoroughly. Continue cooking over high heat for a few seconds, then cover and cook, stirring occasionally - entire cooking time should be 2 minutes, depending on the texture of the spinach.
Makes 3 servings

Spinach, being a light leafy vegetable, requires very little cooking time and no water when being stir-fried. The small amount of water that clings to the leaves after it has been washed is sufficient. If the spinach, after it has been washed, is left out on the counter too long and has become a little dry simply add a tablespoon, or so, of water. You do not want to add too much water or you will be boiling the spinach.

Spinach Stir-Fried with Vegetables

Vegetables can be bought, washed and cut the morning of your meal or even a day ahead of time. After washing your vegetables shake off any excess water then put them in a plastic bag and refrigerate. If the dish calls for meat, poultry or seafood, these too can be cut and refrigerated the day before.

1 pound spinach, washed and trimmed of stems
6 fresh straw mushrooms washed and cut in half, or sliced button mushrooms
1 carrot, sliced
1/2 small can bamboo shoots, rinsed in cold water and drained
3 tablespoons oil
1 teaspoon salt, adjust to taste
1/2 teaspoon white pepper
1 clove garlic, smashed and peeled

Put the oil in a wok that has been placed on medium to high heat, add salt and stir. Add mushrooms, carrot, and bamboo shoots and stir-fry for about 3 minutes. Add spinach and pepper, and stir-fry for an additional 30 seconds. Serve. Makes 4 to 5 servings.

All About Broccoli

In selecting broccoli I usually look at the florets at the top to see if they are nice and green and in snug bunches, and that they are not flowering (this means the flowers are open). I look for stems that are smooth all the way down, with no knots. Then I turn it upside down and look at the bottom of the stem, if the inside, next to the skin, is dry and has a woody appearance it means that it is old. Many people keep the florets and throw the stem away! Don't do that. Every part of the broccoli can be used. When you throw away the stem you are throwing away a lot of food and good vitamins.

Now to prepare the broccoli for cooking. Cut a thin slice off the end, if your fingernail cannot penetrate the skin then the skin should be peeled off. The cooking time is adjusted to the skin, so if it is tough, the cooking time will be longer and the other parts will be over-cooked because they are more tender and require less cooking time. Therefore, if the skin is tough it is necessary to peel it off. To peel the broccoli, hold it upside down and slip a paring knife right under the skin at the end and peel it down just like a banana. If the skin breaks off continue the same way at that point until it reaches close to the bottom of the floret. Peel all around the stem. At certain times of the year the stems are very woody, cut away these parts until the tender part is reached. If the stems are particularly tough cut them in half lengthwise, then cut across the stem into the length you want them. Cut the florets and stems to approximately the same size, so the cooking time will be the same for all parts. If some pieces are much bigger than others, the cooking time will have to be based on the larger pieces. When the large pieces are finally cooked the smaller pieces will be over-cooked. This is why it is so important that you cut the pieces uniformly.

To test if the broccoli is done, get a spatula and press against the stem part with the edge. If the spatula goes through easily then it is done; however if there is a lot of resistance then it is not done yet. When I test it, I simply take a bite to see if it is done. My husband Harry says that a true chef never has to eat the food to tell if it is ready, so I guess I haven't qualified yet!

Stir-fried Broccoli with Bacon

Broccoli is a much harder-bodied vegetable than spinach and may require additional water while stir-frying. The water that is clinging to the florets may be sufficient, but if it is not, get 2 or 3 tablespoons of water and swish it down the sides of the hot wok. The reason for running it down the sides is so the water, when it reaches the rest of the ingredients, will be the same temperature as the ingredients in your wok. If you were to put cold water in the middle of the wok with the other vegetables it would lower the temperature and throw off your cooking time. If the broccoli still isn't cooked enough you may need to add another tablespoon of water down the sides, then cover it immediately so the steam will be contained and cook the vegetable. You can add wine to the dish if you would like instead of water. Swish the wine down the sides as you would with the water. When the wine hits and runs down the hot sides it will sizzle and put forth the most delicious fragrance and will flavor the dish.

1 pound broccoli, sliced or cut into pieces of approximately the same size, drained thoroughly
3 or 4 slices bacon, cut into small pieces
1 clove garlic, smashed
1 small piece of fresh ginger, smashed (about half the size of your thumb)
1/4 teaspoon salt or to taste
1/4 teaspoon sugar
4 tablespoons sherry wine (optional)

Put the bacon pieces in a frying pan or wok over high heat and cook until slightly brown. Add garlic and ginger, and brown them. Add salt, mix. Add broccoli and sugar, and stir-fry over high heat. Swish the wine around down the sides of the wok so it sizzles as it runs into the broccoli. Cover the pan or wok and cook for approximately 3 to 4 minutes until desired tenderness is reached, stirring the broccoli occasionally while cooking. If more liquid is needed, swish 2 or 3 tablespoons down the sides of the wok. Serve immediately. Makes 3 to 4 servings.

Broccoli with Sesame

1 pound fresh broccoli, cut into pieces of
approximately the same size
1 tablespoon toasted sesame seeds, see
page 14
1 teaspoon sugar
1/2 teaspoon sesame oil
1 tablespoon soy sauce
1 3/4 tablespoons wine vinegar

Cook broccoli by steaming it for about 7 to
10 minutes, or until crisp. Combine soy
sauce, vinegar, sugar, and sesame oil in
bowl and mix well. Pour mixture over the
broccoli that has been arranged on a plate,
sprinkle with toasted sesame seeds and
serve. Makes 4 servings.

The most rewarding part of my cooking classes was when my students, after I taught them the stir-fry technique, would tell me how their families were finally starting to eat vegetables happily.

Blanched Gai Lon
Chinese Broccoli

Gai Lon

Gai lon is a slender and tender, deep-green stemmed vegetable with long leaves and often a cluster of small white flowers on the end. It does not require peeling like regular broccoli. Strangely this vegetable is cooked by blanching (boiling briefly). It is a very popular dish in Chinese restaurants, demanding a premium price for just a simply prepared vegetable dish. But it's the technique that counts and not everyone can prepare it properly!

1 pound gai lon (Chinese broccoli)
1 teaspoon salt
1 teaspoon sugar
4 tablespoons cooked oil, see hint opposite page
2 tablespoons oyster sauce, optional

Wash gai lon after trimming yellowed and withered parts, drain. Leave the flowers on. Bring 4 to 5 cups of water to a boil in a 10" frying pan or wok. Add salt, sugar, and 1 1/2 tablespoons of the cooked oil to the boiling water. Add the gai lon, placing it into the water horizontally with the flower ends all in one direction. When the water returns to a boil, blanch the gai long for 30 seconds to 1 minute, depending upon the size of the stems. When gai lon is cooked properly it should be tender but crisp to the bite. Remove immediately by lifting up through the oiled surface of the water with a Chinese bamboo-handled strainer. When it is lifted up through the water in this manner the oil will cling to it and give it an appetizing shine.

Drain the gai lon by shaking the strainer gently then lay the vegetable on a platter, flower ends all in one direction. With kitchen shears, cut through the stems in 2 or

3 pieces. Pour the remaining 2 1/2 tablespoons cooked oil over it evenly and, if
desired, the oyster sauce. Serve immediately. This dish, when done properly, has a
very pretty and appetizing green color.

A Variation
Blanched Yu Choy
Chinese Flowering Cabbage

Another popular vegetable cooked the same
way as the **Blanched Gai Lon** is yu choy
(Chinese flowering cabbage) It is also a
slender green-stemmed vegetable with
larger leaves than the gai lon and with
clusters of small yellow-flowers. As with
the gai lon, leave the flowers on!
Both gai lon and yu choy are usually found
in Chinese stores, but are not available all
year round.

Cooked Oil
*The Chinese often refer to the
cooking oil right out of the
bottle as raw oil. They
therefore cook a large amount
of oil by heating it over high
heat until very hot, this is
"cooked oil." When it cools, it
is stored in a container and
used as needed.*

String Beans with Hot Sesame Sauce

1 pound string beans
3 tablespoons sesame sauce, see recipe below
1 teaspoon salt
1 small piece of ginger, smashed

Remove end-strings from beans, and wash with cold water. Place beans in 2 to 3 cups of boiling water with salt and ginger. Boil for about 2 1/2 minutes. Drain, then blanch with cold water to stop the cooking action. Place beans on a serving plate. Pour sauce over the beans. Serve hot or cold. Make 4 servings.

Hot Sesame Sauce

1 1/2 tablespoons toasted sesame oil
2 tablespoons soy sauce
1/2 teaspoon hot chili oil
1/4 teaspoon salt
1 teaspoon sugar
3 tablespoons water

Mix all of the above ingredients thoroughly. Set aside until ready to use.

Stir-fried Snap Peas

1 pound snap peas
1 teaspoon salt , or to taste
1 clove garlic, smashed and peeled
2 tablespoons water
2 tablespoons oyster sauce, optional

Heat frying pan or wok over high heat. Add oil and heat until very hot. Add salt and stir into oil. Add garlic and brown. Add snap peas and stir-fry over high heat for about 1 minute. Swish 2 tablespoons of water down the sides of the hot wok. Cover wok and cook about 1 minute. Snap peas should be cooked, but crisp to the bite. If the peas are not cooked enough, add 1 more tablespoon of water down the sides of the wok, cover and cook another minute. Add oyster sauce and mix. Serve hot immediately. Serves 4.

Snap peas are relatively new in the grocery stores. They look like peas that are to be shelled but are a little shorter. However, you do not shell snap peas. Remove the tip and pull down the strings. When buying snap peas purchase those that are firm and have a nice, green color.

Braised Bamboo Shoots

1 pound of fresh bamboo shoots
4 ounces lean pork, cut into thin pieces
6 fresh straw mushrooms, washed and
stems removed, cut into thin strips.
2 teaspoons sugar
2 tablespoons soy sauce
5 tablespoons cooking oil
3 teaspoons sesame oil

Cut bamboo shoots into horizontal, 2 inch
long, strips. Place in a bowl with the soy
sauce and sugar. Mix and let stand for 5
minutes, scoop the bamboo shoots out with
a slotted spoon then place pork into the
bowl and mix. Put the cooking oil in a wok
placed on high heat and add bamboo shoots.
Stir-fry bamboo shoots for about 1 minute
and remove. Add mushrooms and pork to
wok and cook for about 1 minute. Add
bamboo shoots to wok and stir-fry for
another minute. Place on warm a plate,
sprinkle with the sesame oil and serve.
Makes 4 to 5 servings.

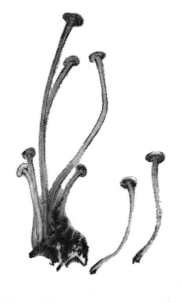

Sesame Cucumber Stir-fry

2 medium sized cucumbers, peeled and
sliced into 1/4" rounds
1 1/2 tablespoons sesame oil
1/4 teaspoon sugar

Heat sesame oil in a wok or frying pan that
has been placed on high heat. Add cucum-
ber pieces and stir-fry for about 1 or 2
minutes. Stir in sugar and serve. Makes 3 to
4 servings.

*Have you ever spent a lot of
time cleaning up the mess
made while peeling or trimming vegetables. You will find
that it takes much less time to
lay out an old newspaper or
opened paper sack, then peel
the vegetables right over it.
When through, just fold up the
newspaper and throw it away!
Less mess, less work!*

All About Bean Sprouts

Bean sprouts that come from mung beans are rich in protein. You can find them in the produce section of the supermarket. In selecting bean sprouts, buy those that are firm and white, not the ones that are brownish or soft. As bean sprouts are sprouted in water they have a high water content; therefore, stir-fry them over high heat and as quickly as possible. The bean sprouts will cook in a very short time, but remain crisp and firm. If you take too long to cook the bean sprouts you will end up with bean threads because they shrivel as the water is cooked out of them. If you have a choice between using the fresh or the can bean sprouts, then by all means use the fresh ones! Canned bean sprouts are not as crisp and taste soggy. Wash the bean sprouts (canned or fresh) in cold water and drain well. Shake off any excess water, and if you are not using them right away, put them in a plastic bag and refrigerate until you need them.

Before removing the bean sprouts from the wok or frying pan, add fresh green onions that have been cut into 1 to 1 1/2 inch pieces. This will add a little color to the bean sprouts, which do not have much color of their own.

Bean Sprout Stir-fry

1 pound bean sprouts
3 small slices fresh ginger
1 clove garlic, smashed and peeled
3 green onions, cut into 1" to 2" pieces
3 tablespoons oil
Salt to taste

Wash bean sprouts, and drain very well.
Heat frying pan or wok over high heat.
Add the oil and heat until very hot. Add
salt and stir it into the oil. Add the garlic
and ginger, browning both. Leave heat on
high and add the bean sprouts. Coat the
bean sprouts thoroughly in the hot oil by
tossing them for approximately 2 to 3
minutes. Just before removing from wok
add the cut green onions, mix. Serve
immediately.

*Smashing the garlic releases
the garlic juice. Do not
smash it into little pieces
unless you plan to mince it,
or if you like to eat the little
browned pieces.*

All About Zucchini

The rule of thumb is that a younger vegetable cooks quickly and an older vegetable takes longer to cook. Zucchini is the opposite! This is because young zucchini are quite solid and the older ones are rather soft. For that matter, sometimes when I get one of those 5 or 6 pound zucchini, I peel it and scrap out the seeds and fibers. It is often soft so that it needs very little cooking.

If zucchini is young then leave the peel on, if desired. If the zucchini is big and old then test it with your fingernail. If the skin is difficult to penetrate with your fingernail then peel it and use a tablespoon to scrape out all the big seeds inside before cutting and cooking.

Zucchini is one of the vegetables that I use quite often when I make my appearances. I recall one time when I went to a supermarket to do a demonstration, the manager asked what I was going to stir-fry. I answered "zucchini," and the manager said, "ugh, I do not like zucchini." But he tried it and liked it so well that each time I made it, he was right there to get some more! It is a rather bland vegetable, so I like to stir-fry it with bacon, when it is done in this way the dish gives off a delicious aroma.

Whenever I serve stir-fry zucchini many people are surprised at how crunchy it is. They usually think of cooked zucchini as being soft and mushy as a result of the cooking methods used. This crunchiness is the result of the stir-fry method. Zucchini has a high water content so little, if any, water will need be added. But you will find that the older zucchini as it is much softer by nature will not be as crunchy as the younger ones.

Stir-fried Zucchini with Bacon and Foo Yee

1 pound zucchini, peeled and cut into
chunks (leave peel on, if desired)
3 or 4 slices bacon, cut into small pieces
1 clove garlic, mashed
Salt to taste (1/4 teaspoon)
1/4 teaspoon sugar
1 preserved cake foo yee, mashed,
see page 177

Put the bacon pieces in a frying pan and
cook over high heat until slightly brown. If
there is too much bacon grease, pour off
excess and save for another dish. Add salt
and garlic. After the garlic has been
browned, add the foo yee and stir into the
hot oil, then add zucchini and sugar, mix
well. Cover and cook over high heat,
stirring occasionally, for about 2 minutes.
Remember the high heat must be constant
until the food is removed from the wok.
Makes 3 to 4 servings.

*It is very important to stir-fry
the foo yee in the hot oil in the
frying pan or wok. This
technique adds an extra special
fragrance and flavor to the dish
and separates the dishwasher
cook from the master chef.
When you add the foo yee to
the hot oil you may remove the
pan from the heat momentarily
as it will cause some splattering. After mixing put the wok
back on the heat immediately,
add your zucchini and
continue to stir-fry.*

Stir-fried Iceberg Lettuce with Oyster Sauce

1 head iceberg lettuce, washed, drained
thoroughly, separated, broken into large
pieces and left at room temperature
4 tablespoons cooking oil
1 clove garlic, smashed
1/2 teaspoon salt, or to taste
1/4 sugar
3 tablespoons oyster sauce, optional

Heat the frying pan or wok over high heat.
Add the oil and heat until very hot. Add the
salt, then the garlic. Brown the garlic. Add
the iceberg lettuce and toss thoroughly.
Cook approximately 2 minutes. Add sugar
and oyster sauce. Toss thoroughly. Remove
to serving plate and serve immediately.
Lettuce should be shriveled only slightly,
but still have body. Serves 4.

Stir-fried Bok Choy

1 1/2 pounds bok choy, washed and cut diagonally into 1" to 1 1/2" thick pieces, drained thoroughly
1 small piece of fresh ginger, smashed
1 clove garlic, smashed and peeled
3 tablespoons cooking oil
1 teaspoon salt, or to taste
2 tablespoons water or sherry wine

Heat frying pan or wok over high heat. Add oil and heat until very hot. Add salt and stir it into the hot oil. Add garlic and ginger, browning it by stir-frying over high heat for about 1 minute. Add bok choy and stir-fry for about 2 minutes. Swish the 2 tablespoons of water or sherry down the hot sides of the wok. Cover the wok and cook for 1 minute. Lift the cover and briefly stir-fry. If the bok choy is not cooked enough for your taste, swish another tablespoon or two of liquid down the sides. Serve immediately.

Bok Choy, known as Chinese white cabbage or Chinese chard, is one of the most common of all Chinese vegetables. It is available year round in grocery stores. The stalks are thicker than nappa cabbage and are white. Bok choy is excellent for stir-frying alone or mixed with other vegetables. Select those bok choy that that have firm stalks and fresh-looking leaves.

For cutting your vegetables, such as green onions or bok choy, celery, or any stalky vegetable, don't cut them one stalk at a time! Lay 4 or 5 stalks together, or as many as your hand can handle comfortably, then cut across the whole bunch. This way you will save a lot of time.

All About Mushrooms, Water Chestnuts, and Sugar Peas

Mushrooms

In selecting white mushrooms, get the ones that are very white. It is important that you turn the mushroom upside down and look at the underside of the cap, it should be tightly closed, if it is opened a little that means that the mushroom has been sitting around in the produce section for a while. The tightly closed ones are the fresh ones. I usually try to select the mushrooms that have a very short stem, although the stems are perfectly edible, I prefer more of the mushroom cap and they all cost the same so why not select the ones that have more cap to them? Do not soak the mushrooms in water to wash them. Hold them under running water, the cap side up, and with your thumb slowly rub around to remove any excess dirt (I think a mushroom brush is unnecessary), then rinse the bottom very briefly before draining thoroughly. You don't want the mushrooms to absorb any water as mushrooms already contain a large amount of water, by adding more to them it could throw off your cooking time while stir-frying. When you slice a mushroom cut it at least a quarter inch thick, if they are small leave them whole. Stir-fry mushrooms very quickly as the longer you cook them the more water will come out and dilute the taste.

Water Chestnuts

Canned water chestnuts are packed in water in flat tins that run from 4 to 6 ounces per tin. Go to a Chinese store to get them, they are cheaper there. Water chestnuts all come from the same place, but for some reason the ones with an oriental name on them are less expensive! It is important that you throw away the water that the chestnuts are packed in as it has a little off-flavor to it. Rinse the water chestnuts several times and drain them thoroughly. Water chestnuts come whole, sliced, or diced. In most of the recipes that call for stir-frying, sliced water chestnuts are used. If you have never tasted a fresh water chestnut you don't know what you are missing. The fresh ones are really delicious and very sweet! It is the same thing as eating a fresh apple versus an apple that has been canned. The water in the can steeps all the flavor out of the water chestnut, therefore it has very little taste. The main reason you are using it is for its crunchiness. No matter how much you cook a water chestnut it remains crunchy; it gives a nutty texture to a dish. Fresh water chestnuts can be bought from Chinese stores, but you don't often see them. They look like little round balls and are about 1 inch in diameter with a dark brown skin. The fresh ones must be peeled, washed, and sliced. Do not soak the fresh ones in water!

Sugar peas

In selecting sugar peas buy those that are nicely green and the peas inside have hardly formed. When the peas inside are large that means that the pea pod is getting old and will be tougher than the younger ones. The frozen sugar peas do not have the same crispness as the fresh ones, because they have been blanched prior to being frozen. You have to take this into consideration when you stir-fry them; really, all you want to do with the frozen ones is warm them not cook them.

Stir-fried Sugar Peas with Peppers, Mushrooms, Water Chestnuts, and Oyster Sauce

The various peppers add a lot of color to this dish.

Sugar peas require a little more cooking time, that is why I add them first. People are used to eating peppers raw, so it is nice to keep them crunchy; cooking them enough to just get them hot is sufficient.

Even after a stir-fried dish is taken from the wok and put in a serving bowl, it continues to cook. You will learn from experience how to time cooking your vegetables. My greatest downfall is when I cook sugar peas. They are nice and crisp when I scoop them into a bowl, but then they stand there waiting to be served. When I dish them up the top pea pods are crunchy however the ones underneath have continued to cook and are not as crisp! This is always a disappointment.

1/2 pound sugar peas, strings removed, washed, and drained thoroughly
1 small green pepper
1 small red pepper
1 small yellow pepper
1/2 cup sliced canned water chestnuts, rinsed and drained
1/2 cup sliced fresh mushrooms (more, if desired)
1 clove garlic, smashed and peeled
1 teaspoon salt, or to taste
1/2 teaspoon sugar
2 tablespoon oyster sauce, optional

Heat frying pan or wok over high heat. Add oil and heat until very hot. Add salt, stir into hot oil. Add garlic and brown. Add sugar peas and stir-fry over high heat for 1 minute. Then add the rest of the ingredients and continue stir-frying over high heat. If needed, swish 1 to 2 tablespoons of water down the sides and continue cooking for 1 minute. Mix in oyster sauce just before serving. Serve immediately. Serves 4 to 6.

Stir-fried Green Peppers with Hot Chili Sauce

4 medium green peppers, cut into approximately 1 1/2" pieces after removing the stems and seeds
3 tablespoons oil
1 teaspoon salt, or to taste
1/2 teaspoon sugar
1 clove garlic, smashed
Hot chili oil to taste, see recipe page 177
2 tablespoons sherry wine (optional)

Heat the frying pan or wok over high heat, add the oil, and heat until very hot. Add the salt and stir. Add the garlic and brown on both sides. Add the cut green peppers and sugar. Toss thoroughly. If needed add 2 tablespoons sherry wine or water by swishing it down the sides of the wok. Cover so the steam can permeate through the vegetable and cook them. Total cooking time is approximately 2 minutes, depending on how crispy you like your peppers. Add hot chili oil and toss thoroughly. Serve immediately. Serves 4.

I like to cut my vegetables into different shapes — 3, 4, 5 and 6 sided shapes. This adds more visual interest to the dish. When I cut it all the same size, it reminds me of dishes bought from the frozen food department. When you serve good home-cooked food you want it to look like good home-cooked food. Remember appearance and color make a lot of difference because you eat with your eyes before your mouth.

All About Asparagus

Fresh asparagus is another vegetable that is very delicious stir-fried. In selecting asparagus buy those spears that are nice and firm and not opened. Buy stalks that are green all the way down, or as far down as possible, because if there is too much white you have to snap it off. To know which part of the asparagus to throw away go along the stalk with both hands bending it slightly, there is a natural breaking point between the tender part and the woody part. You may have noticed how in some stores asparagus costs a lot more than in others, but look at the asparagus, if a large part of the stem is white you will have to throw that away, whereas generally the more expensive asparagus is green and edible all the way down. Wash the asparagus and drain thoroughly, then cut it diagonally into 1/2 inch slices or leave them whole. I prefer to cut my asparagus into only 2 or 3 pieces, but if you are serving a lot of people and want to stretch on the asparagus, simply cut it into smaller pieces. Regardless of how you cut it, be sure that all the pieces are of approximately the same size so they will cook evenly.

Stir-fry the asparagus for about as long as you would broccoli, approximately 2 to 3 minutes, depending on how old it is and how big the pieces are. You can substitute asparagus for broccoli in any of these recipes. It is also very delicious simply stir-fried in oil with a little garlic. Or just before you are ready to take it out of the wok, add a tablespoon or so of oyster sauce and toss, then serve immediately. This is one dish for which I am sure you will get a lots of raves!

Stir-fried Asparagus with Oyster Sauce

1 pound asparagus, snapped at the natural
breaking point, washed, drained and cut
diagonally into 1" pieces.
3 tablespoons oil
1/2 teaspoon salt
1 clove garlic, smashed and peeled
1/2 teaspoon sugar
3 tablespoons oyster sauce
3 tablespoons water or sherry vinegar

Put a pan or wok over high heat, add oil and
heat until hot. Add salt and stir. Add garlic
and brown. Add asparagus and stir-fry over
continuous high heat for 1 minute. Swish
the water or sherry wine around down the
hot sides of the wok so it sizzles as it runs
down into the asparagus. Cover and cook
another minute. Add oyster sauce and
sugar. Mix thoroughly. Serve hot, immediately. Serves 4.

*For those people who are on a
salt-free diet, simply delete the
salt and it will still turn out
very delicious.*

Chapter Four
Fish and Shellfish

Fish and Shellfish

Deep-fried Shrimp

1 pound large uncooked shrimp, shelled and
butterflied, see page 98
2 teaspoons soy sauce
1 tablespoon sherry wine
1 small clove garlic, minced
1/4 teaspoon salt
1/4 teaspoon sesame oil
1/4 teaspoon sugar
1/2 teaspoon minced fresh ginger
Basic batter, see recipe page 168
Oil for deep-frying shrimp

Mix the soy sauce, wine, ginger, garlic, salt,
sesame oil, and sugar; add the shrimp.
Marinate the shrimp for at least 30 minutes.
Heat the oil to 375 degrees. Remove the
shrimp from marinade and drain. Dip each
shrimp into the batter. Deep fry one at a
time, waiting for the batter to sizzle and set
before adding the next shrimp. Cook until a
golden brown color, remove immediately,
drain, and serve with hot red sauce (ketchup
mixed with Chinese hot mustard). Makes 3
to 4 servings.

*Do not be impatient when
putting the shrimp into the hot
oil. If you put them in all at
once, instead of one by one,
they will form a big glob. Wait
until each shrimp sets in its
batter before adding the next
shrimp.*

Hot Red Sauce
*Many people have asked how
to make the delicious, hot red
sauce that is found in Chinese
restaurants. It is simply
ketchup with the Chinese
mustard mixed in.*

Shrimp with Tomato Sauce

To butterfly the shrimp, split them down the middle from top to bottom, almost all the way through the center, but not all the way — just enough so they open to form a butterfly! I find it easiest to curve the shrimp into a ball, with the back facing towards me, then cut down the middle from top to bottom. The reason for butterflying the shrimp is so that the heat can get inside and cook it all the way through. Also deep-fried butterflied shrimp give the illusion of being really big shrimp. The bigger the shrimp the more they cost per pound, and the larger ones don't taste any better, so butterflying the smaller ones is a nice way to stretch your shrimpy budget! The shrimp that come 30 to 35 per pound are a nice size.

1 pound uncooked shrimp, shelled, drained and butterflied
5 tablespoons oil
1/2 teaspoon salt
1 clove garlic, smashed and peeled
3 tablespoons sherry wine
Dash of white pepper
1 small piece ginger, smashed
4 tablespoons tomato ketchup
1/2 cup basic soup stock, see recipe page 169
1/2 tablespoon cornstarch mixed with 1/2 tablespoon cold water
4 green onions, cut into 1 1/2" lengths

Put 3 1/2 tablespoons of the oil in a frying pan that has been set over high heat. When hot, add salt and garlic. Brown garlic, then add shrimp and stir-fry over high heat for about 1 minute. Swish in the sherry wine sizzling down the hot sides of the wok. Add the pepper and stir-fry 1 more minute. Remove shrimp to a dish. Put remaining oil in that wok that has been set over high heat. Heat oil until hot. Add ginger and stir briskly. Add tomato ketchup and stir while it sizzles in the hot oil. Then add soup stock. Bring to a boil. Slowly stir in cornstarch mixture until liquid thickens. Return shrimp and add green onions. Mix briskly, serve immediately. Serves 3 to 4.

A Wok with Mary Pang

Stir-fried Abalone with Oyster Sauce

1 pound fresh abalone, pounded to tender-
ize. Cut into slices approximately 1/4"
thick, 1" wide, and 2" long. Save the liquid
from pounding for cooking.
4 tablespoons oil
1/4 teaspoon salt, or to taste
1 clove garlic, smashed and peeled
1 small piece ginger, smashed
3 tablespoons oyster sauce
2 tablespoons sherry wine
enough water added to the abalone liquid to
make approximately 1/3 cup liquid
1/2 teaspoon sugar
1/2 tablespoon cornstarch mixed with 1/2
tablespoon cold water
3 green onions, cut into 1/2" pieces

Place wok or frying pan over high heat.
Add 3 tablespoon oil and heat until hot.
Add salt; stir. Add garlic and ginger, and
brown. Add abalone and quickly stir-fry
over high heat for 1/2 minute. Remove
immediately to a dish. Add remaining 1 tablespoon of oil and heat until hot. Remove
pan from heat, then add oyster sauce and
sherry wine, and swish around in the hot
oil. Return wok to heat, add 1/3 cup of
liquid and sugar. When boiling, take wok
off the heat and slowly stir in cornstarch
mixture until desired thickness is reached.
Return to heat. Add cooked abalone and
green onions. Mix. Serve immediately.

*Timing is very important in
this dish. Over-cooking will
toughen the abalone.*

*The reason you remove the pan
with the hot oil from the heat
before you add the oyster sauce
is that it spatters all over. This
technique keeps most of the
oyster sauce in the pan and
saves on clean-up. It is still
hot enough and you will get
that sizzle that you need. This
method adds more fragrance
and taste to the dish.*

Stir-fried Clams in Their Shells

25 small steamer clams, washed
4 tablespoons oil
2 cloves garlic, smashed and peeled
1 small piece ginger, smashed
1 small onion, cut into wedges
1/2 teaspoon salt
1/4 teaspoon sugar
3 tablespoons sherry wine
4 green onions, cut into 1 1/2" lengths

Soup stock or water can always be substituted for sherry wine.

Add oil to wok or frying pan over high heat. Heat until hot. Add salt and stir. Add garlic and ginger and brown. Add clams and sugar and mix thoroughly. Swish sherry wine down the hot sides of wok. Cover, turn heat down to medium-high. Cook for approximately 4 to 5 minutes. When shells are all opened, the dish is cooked. Add green onion and toss thoroughly. Serve immediately. Serves 4 to 5.

Stir-fried Dungeness Crab with Black Bean Sauce

1 large, fresh Dungeness crab, cleaned. Remove shell and save crab fat. Disjoint and crack legs and claws; cut body parts into 3 pieces each.
3 tablespoons oil
1/2 teaspoon salt
1 clove garlic, smashed and peeled
1 1/2 tablespoons black bean sauce
4 tablespoons sherry wine
1 cup basic soup stock, see recipe page 169
1 egg, beaten
1/2 tablespoon cornstarch mixed with 1/2 tablespoon water
4 green onions, cut into 2" lengths

Heat wok or frying pan over high heat. Add oil and heat until very hot. Add salt and stir. Add garlic and brown. Carefully add black bean sauce and mix. (Be sure to be careful as it will splatter.) Then immediately add Dungeness crab. Toss and mix thoroughly over high heat. Swish sherry wine down the hot sides of the wok. Toss crab again, then swish soup stock down hot sides. Cover and cook over high heat for approximately 3 to 4 minutes. Soup stock should be boiling vigorously. Mix in crab fat and heat. Gradually stir in beaten egg. Then slowly stir in cornstarch mixture until desired thickness is reached. It should be a medium-thin sauce. Turn and mix everything until sauce is fully cooked and hot, this will take about 1/2 minute. Add green onions and mix well. Serve immediately. Serves 2 to 3.

This sauce is delicious over hot steamed rice.

This is one time that using your fingers is a must! It's messy, but worth it.

Stir-fried Lobster with Vegetables

Meat from 2 lobster tails, approximately 1
pound of meat, sliced into 1/2" pieces
5 tablespoons oil
1 teaspoon salt, or to taste
1 tablespoons sherry wine
1 garlic clove, smashed and peeled
1 small piece ginger, smashed
1/4 pound sugar peas, tips and strings
removed, washed, and drained
1/2 cup sliced celery, 1/8" thick
1 small can button mushrooms, drained
3 tablespoons oyster sauce
1/2 cup basic soup stock, see page 169
1/2 teaspoon sugar
1/2 tablespoon cornstarch mixed with 1/2
tablespoon cold water
4 green onions, cut into 1 1/2" pieces

*Since most stir-fry dishes
must be served immediately
after being cooked, most
people are apprehensive that
they will not be able to handle
the situation. However, with
preparation and practice
everything will run smoothly
and you will be proud of the
food you serve.*

Heat wok or frying pan over high heat. Add
2 of the tablespoons of oil and heat until
very hot. Add 1/2 teaspoon of salt and stir.
Add garlic and ginger, and brown. Add
lobster meat and stir-fry over high heat for 1
minute. Swish sherry wine down hot sides
of wok. Cover and cook 1 more minute.
Toss thoroughly; remove to a dish.

Heat wok over high heat, add 1 1/2 tablespoons of the oil. Heat until hot. Add

remaining 1/2 teaspoon salt and stir into hot oil. Add vegetables (sugar peas, mushrooms, celery, and water chestnuts). Stir-fry over high heat for 1 minute. Swish 2 tablespoons water sizzling down the hot sides of the wok. Cover and cook 1/2 minute. Toss thoroughly. Remove to a dish.

Add remaining oil to wok and heat until hot. Remove wok from heat and swish in oyster sauce so it sizzles in the hot oil. Return to heat and add soup stock and sugar. Heat until boiling. Slowly stir in the cornstarch mixture until soup stock thickens and is boiling. Add lobster, vegetables, and green onions. Mix briskly for 1/2 minute to heat. Serve immediately. Serves 4 to 5.

Do not be afraid to experiment. Substitute other vegetables here, if you want. the technique is the same.

Stir-fried Scallops with Ginger

1 pound fresh medium scallops, washed and drained
3 tablespoons oil
1/2 teaspoon salt, or to taste
1 clove garlic, smashed and peeled
5 thin slices of fresh ginger, cut into thin strips
1/2 teaspoon sugar
4 tablespoons sherry wine (water can be substituted)
4 green onions, cut into 1 1/2" lengths

Do not over-cook scallops — they will become tough.

Put wok or frying pan over high heat. Add oil and heat until hot. Add salt and stir. Add garlic and brown. Add ginger and stir-fry until you can detect ginger aroma rising. Immediately add scallops and sugar, and stir-fry over high heat for 1 1/2 minutes. Swish the sherry wine sizzling down the hot sides of the wok. Cover and cook another minute. When the scallops are cooked they loose their translucent appearance and become white. Add green onions, mix. Serve immediately.

Fish Fillets

1/2 pound fish fillets, (your choice),
cut into 1 1/2 by 2 inch strips
2 tablespoons sherry
1/2 teaspoon salt
1/4 teaspoon white pepper
1 egg white, beaten
Vegetable oil for deep frying
1 cup cornstarch

Mix sherry, salt, and white pepper in a
bowl, drag fish through mixture to thoroughly coat, then dredge in cornstarch.
Combine remaining cornstarch and egg, and
coat dredged fish in this mixture. Heat 3
inches of oil in a frying pan to 350°, and
cook fish a few pieces at a time, placing fish
on paper towels to drain. Makes 3 servings.

*If you use fillet of sole, handle
it very gently, as it is such a
delicate fish.*

Chow Yee Peen
Fish Fillets with Bean Sprouts

I have formed a habit of using a plate right by the stove. I use a six inch saucer and on it I put my chop sticks, spoon, etc. so that every time I put these things down I know where they are, plus they are not getting the counter messy. Taking a dirty plate to the sink to wash is easier than cleaning a counter that is dirty here and there. You don't need one of those special spoon holders. They are too small anyway, a regular plate really works better. This helps keep your counter more organized and clean.

1 pound fish (rock cod, sturgeon, striped bass or halibut) cut in 1/4-inch thick slices, 1 1/2" long, 1" wide
4 tablespoon cornstarch

Marinade:
1/2 teaspoon soy sauce
1 clove garlic, minced
1 slice fresh ginger, minced
1/4 teaspoon sugar
1 teaspoon sherry wine
1/2 teaspoon sesame oil
1/4 teaspoon salt
1/2 tablespoon oyster sauce
1 teaspoon minced green onions
1 tablespoon oil
Dash of black pepper

Combine marinade ingredients. Sprinkle over fish slices. Toss gently to coat thoroughly. Then sprinkle cornstarch over marinated fish slices. Mix gently to coat. Set aside until ready to cook.

4 tablespoons oil
1 pound bean sprouts
1/4 teaspoon salt
1 clove garlic, smashed and peeled
2 small slices fresh ginger, slivered
1 tablespoon oyster sauce
2 green onions, cut into 1" lengths

You will notice that in many of these fish recipes I use a combination of garlic, ginger and sherry wine. This trio helps to counteract any strong fish taste.

Place 1 tablespoon oil in a frying pan that has been placed over high heat. When the oil is hot add the salt, garlic, and ginger. Stir until garlic is lightly browned and then add bean sprouts. Continue to stir-fry for 1 minute. Add the oyster sauce and green onions and mix. Remove to a serving dish. In a frying pan place the remaining 4 table-spoons of oil and set over high heat. When hot, add the marinated fish slices and brown on both sides. Place the fish on top of the stir-fry bean sprouts and serve. Makes 3 to 4 servings.

When turning the slices of fish in the frying pan to brown on the other side, flip them over with a spatula, like a pancake. Lift browned slices of fish out with the spatula also, as they may break easily.

Steamed Fish with Black Bean Sauce

The cooking time for steamed fish is figured at approximately 8 to 10 minutes per inch thick of fish. Take the fish out of the refrigerator about half and hour before steaming. If you steam it directly from the refrigerator is will throw off your cooking time.

2 slices of 3/4 inch thick fish
1 1/2 tablespoons black bean sauce, see recipe page 171
Salt to taste
1 green onion, cut into 1 1/2" lengths, then cut into strips lengthwise
2 tablespoons oil

Place slices of fish in a shallow dish and salt to taste. Spread black bean sauce evenly over fish. Place in a fish steamer (see steaming instructions, page 11). Cover pan and cook vigorously, steaming the fish for about 6 to 10 minutes. Sprinkle green onions on top. Heat oil in a small saucepan until very hot. Pour evenly over the fish and green onions. If possible, pour the oil at arms' length, as it will splatter. Before serving, spoon the hot liquid over the fish few times. Serves 2.

The hot oil that is poured over the fish imparts a very fragrant taste. If, however, you don't care for the oil you can leave it out. But I think that it adds a very special taste.

Steamed Rock Cod

1 rock cod, 1 1/2 to 2 1/2 pounds, cleaned
with the head left on
1/2 teaspoon salt
1/4 teaspoon sugar
6 green onions, cut into 2" lengths with the
white parts cut thin lengthwise.
6 slices fresh ginger, cut into thin strips
5 tablespoons peanut oil
1 teaspoon sesame oil
2 1/2 tablespoons soy sauce

Make 3 deep, diagonal slashes on both sides
of the fish. Place fish into an oven-proof dish
and steam fish on high heat in a wok or in a
steamer for about 20 to 25 minutes, with the
cover on. Remove cover, sprinkle fish on
both sides with salt and sugar then spread
top evenly with ginger and green onions.
Heat the peanut oil in small pan set over
high heat until very hot. Pour it slowly and
evenly over entire fish. Remove dish from
wok or steamer. Sprinkle with soy sauce and
sesame oil. Before serving pour seasoned
liquid in dish over the fish a few times.
Serve hot. Makes 4 to 5 servings.

*If available, sea bass is great.
The diagonal slashes cut deep
into the sides of the fish
enables the heat to get in and
cook the fish evenly, inside
and out. Without the slashes
the outside of the fish will be
overcooked by the time the
inside parts are done.*

*To test if the fish is cooked,
poke a chopstick into the thick
portion of the fish. If the
chopstick goes in easily, its
done. If the chopstick meets
with resistance then it needs
more cooking. Remove the fish
immediately from the steamer
when it is done. There is quite
a bit of retained heat within the
steamer that will continue to
cook the fish if you leave it
there. Remember — do not
over cook. Practice makes
perfect!*

Chapter Five
Chicken and Meat

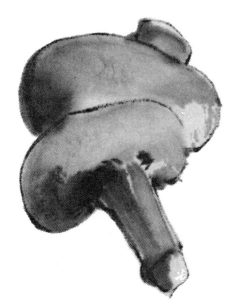

Chicken

Chicken and Bean Sprout Stir-Fry

1/2 pound chicken breast, boned, skinned,
and shredded
1 teaspoon oyster sauce
2 teaspoons light soy sauce
1/4 teaspoon salt, or to taste
1/8 teaspoon sugar
1 tablespoon sherry wine
2 tablespoons cornstarch
5 tablespoons oil
1 clove garlic, smashed and peeled
3 thin slices ginger, cut into thin strips
1 1/2 pounds bean sprouts, rinsed and
drained
1/2 teaspoon sugar
3 green onions, cut into 1" lengths

Mix together the chicken, oyster sauce, soy
sauce, salt, sugar, and sherry wine. Add oil
and mix. Add cornstarch and mix. Put
frying pan or wok over high heat. Add
2 1/2 tablespoons oil. Heat until very hot.
Add marinated chicken and spread over the
bottom of the pan. Fry for 1 minute, or until
brown. Flip the chicken over like a pancake.
Continue frying for another minute. Then
stir-fry for 1/2 minute. Remove to a separate dish. Put remaining oil into hot pan
over high heat. Heat until hot. Add salt and
stir. Add garlic and brown. Add ginger
strips and stir until you smell the fragrance
of the ginger. Add drained bean sprouts
and sugar, and stir-fry for 1 minute over
high heat. Add cooked chiken and cut
green onions, and mix briskly. Put into
serving dish and serve hot. Serves 2 to 3.

*I have noticed many people
wipe their hands on cloth
kitchen towels after cutting
raw meat, then hang the towels
on a rack. Then they wipe
their hands on the same towel
before they cut the cooked dish.
This is a very good way of
getting food poisoning. I use
paper towels and throw them
away. I realize this is a bit
costly, but it isn't as expensive
as going to the doctor for food
poisoning!*

Cashew Chicken

Light soy sauce is light in color and is often used for flavoring chicken so as not to darken it. It has a very delicious fragrance of its own. It is also salty.

1 chicken breast, boned and cut into 1/4" thick slices
1 tablespoon light soy sauce
1/4 teaspoon salt, or to taste
1/8 teaspoon sugar
1 tablespoon sherry wine
1 1/2 tablespoon oil
2 1/2 tablespoons cornstarch
5 tablespoons oil
2 tablespoons oyster sauce mixed with 1/4 teaspoon sugar
1/2 cup basic soup stock, see page 169
4 green onions, cut into 1 1/2" lengths
1 tablespoon cornstarch mixed with
1 tablespoon cold water
1 cup raw cashews, deep-fried

Mix together chicken, light soy sauce, salt, sugar, and sherry wine. Add oil and mix. Add cornstarch and mix. Put frying pan or wok over high heat. Add 3 tablespoons oil. Heat until very hot. Add marinated chicken and spread over bottom of pan. Fry over high for 1 minute until brown. Flip over like a pancake. Continue frying for 1 minute, or until brown, then stir briskly for 1/2 minute. Remove to a separate dish. Put remaining oil in hot pan over high heat. Heat until hot. Remove from burner, add oyster sauce and sugar. Mix into hot oil. Return pan to high heat and stir a few seconds until oyster sauce sizzles. Add soup stock and bring to a boil. Gradually add cornstarch mixture until desired thickness is reached. Add cooked chicken, deep- fried cashews and cut green onons. Mix briskly for 1/2 minute. Serve immediately. Serves 2 to 3.

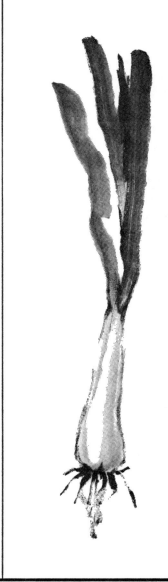

Steamed Chicken with Gum Jum

1/2 pound chicken meat, cut into slices
1 teaspoon soy sauce
1/4 teaspoon salt
1 teaspoon oyster sauce
1 teaspoon sherry wine
1/4 teaspoon sugar
1 tablespoon oil
4 teaspoons cornstarch

Mix together the chicken, soy sauce, salt, oyster sauce, sherry wine, and sugar. Add oil and mix. Add cornstarch and mix. Marinate chicken for 15 minutes. Place in a shallow dish that is large enough to hold chicken and the ingredients listed below:

1/3 cup of gum jum (lily flowers) soaked, drained, and squeezed
8 small black mushrooms, soaked, drained, and cut into strips
2 Chinese dried red dates (hoong jo) soaked, drained, and cut into strips
4 water chestnuts, rinsed, drained and cut into strips
1 small fresh ginger, thinly sliced
1/2 Chinese sausage, cut into strips
A few drops of sesame oil
Sliced green onions and parsley as garnish

Black Mushrooms
These dried mushrooms come from Japan. They can be found in Chinese stores and many supermarkets. Soak them for 20 minutes, then remove the stems.

Hoong Jo
These are dried red dates from China. They are better and sweeter than the dates grown in the United States.

Chinese Sausage
These sausages are found in Chinese stores. They should be cooked before the are eaten.

Spread ingredients over the chicken pieces. Steam (see steaming instructions page 11) over high heat for about 20 minutes. Remove dish from pan and top with sliced green onions and parsley. Makes 3 to 4 servings.

Chicken Steamed with Szechwan Preserved Vegetables

Szechwan preserved vegetable
This is a vegetable that has been preserved in salt and pickled with chili powder. It has an interesting, hot bite to it. It comes in a can and may be purchased at a Chinese store. After opening the can transfer the contents to a bottle with a tight lid and refrigerate. The vegetables come in big chunks, simply cut off what you need. You can steam it with sliced meat, stir-fry it and even put it in soups. Put it in a soup recipe just long enough to heat it through and to bring out its hot flavor. Or eat it sliced, cold. The chili powder can be rinsed off, but leaving it on gives it a much better, hot taste. It is quite salty.

1/2 pound chicken breast, boned, and sliced 1/4" thick
2 teaspoons light soy sauce
1/8 teaspoon salt, or to taste
1 tablespoon sherry wine (optional)
1 tablespoon oil
1 1/2 tablespoon cornstarch
1/3 cup Szechwan preserved vegetables, sliced into thin pieces
1 green onion, cut into 1" lengths
1 1/2 tablespoon oil

Mix together chicken, soy sauce, salt, sugar, and sherry wine. Add oil and mix. Add cornstarch and mix. Place marinated chicken into ovenproof dish. Spread chicken evenly over bottom of dish. Sprinkle thin pieces of Szechwan preserved vegetables over surface. Place in steamer when water is boiling. Steam for 20 minutes, or until done. Remove from steamer immediately. Sprinkle green onions over surface. Heat oil in pan until very hot. Pour over surface of steamed chicken and green onoins. Serve immediately. Serves 2.

Chinese-Style Roast Chicken

1 young fryer, about 3 pounds
salt to taste
2 cups basic soy sauce seasoning, see recipe
page 167

Rub the chicken inside and out with the
basic soy sauce seasoning, then salt lightly
inside and out, and let stand overnight in
pan in refrigerator. Remove from refrigerator about 2 hours before roasting. Truss
wings and tie loosely. Set chicken, back side
up, on a wire rack in a foil lined pan. Put in
a preheated 450 degree oven. Roast 15
minutes, then turn heat down to 350 degrees, and continue roasting for 40 minutes.
When chicken is nicely browned, take out of
oven and brush with basic soy sauce seasoning, to which a little oil has been added.
Turn chicken, breast side up, and brush
again with soy sauce and oil. Continue
roasting, breast side up, until done. Brush
once more with soy sauce and oil. Total
cooking time is approximately 50 to 55
minutes.

*The chicken is put on the oiled
wire rack, back side up first,
because the fat under the skin
of the back will baste the
chicken sides and breast as it
melts and flows downwards.
As a result, the breast meat
will be more moist and tender
— an important technique to
remember.*

*If two chickens are placed on
the rack to be roasted increase
the cooking time by about 5 to
7 minutes.*

*It is best to take the chicken out
of the oven and baste it
thoroughly. But, remember to
add on that time to the overall
cooking time. And to shut the
oven door each time, otherwise,
the oven will cool considerably.*

*Let the chicken rest for about
20 minutes before carving it,
or all the juices will flow out.
In addition, it is easier to cut
after it has cooled a bit.*

Chinese-Style Fried Chicken with Soy Sauce

The cutting board is a hotbed for food poisoning. Say you were cooking fried chicken that you cut on the cutting board that you wipe dry. Then you decide to have a nice green salad and cut your vegetables on the same board. That is very dangerous. You are contaminating your vegetables. I usually wash my vegetables first, drain them, then cut the chicken afterwards. If you do cut the chicken first, be sure you wash the board and knife thoroughly with soap and hot water and rinse them well. Remember to scrub your hands with plenty of soap and hot water. That is a source of transferring contaminated diseases.

2 pounds chicken wings, disjointed,
5 tablespoons cooking oil
Basic soy sauce seasoning, see recipe
page 167
Salt to taste

Heat oil in a frying pan. When oil is hot, put in the pieces of chicken and fry on both sides until brown. Pour off excess oil. Mix 1/4 cup of soy sauce seasoning with 1/4 cup of water and pour this mixture over the chicken. Turn the heat down when you pour the sauce in or it will burn. Cover and cook slowly, turning pieces occasionally. Cook 20 minutes or until done. If the sauce is too thick at the end of the cooking period, add a little water. Makes 3 to 4 servings.

Almond Chicken

2 boned chicken breasts, cut into fillets
1 to 2 cups thick basic batter, see recipe
page 168
1 cup toasted almonds, finely chopped
Chinese-style brown gravy, see recipe
page 172
1/4 head lettuce, shredded
Oil for deep-frying chicken

Mix 1/4 cup almonds into the batter, then dip in the chicken fillets. Deep-fry both in oil heated to 350 degrees until golden brown, drain, and cut into slices. Arrange these on a bed of shredded lettuce. Pour the hot Chinese-style brown gravy over chicken. Garnish with remaining almonds. Makes 4 to 6 servings.

The battered chicken fillet can be deep-fried a light brown ahead of time and refrigerated until ready to be served. Then deep fry it for a second time to further brown it and re-crisp. Do not pour hot Chinese style gravy over hot deep-fried chicken until ready to serve. If you do this too far ahead of time it will lose its crispness. The deep-fried chicken fillets can also be frozen for future use. But, thaw before deep frying.

Chicken and Water Chestnut Skewers

1/2 pound boned chicken breasts
8 water chestnuts, rinsed, and drained, and
cut into 3 thick slices each
1/2 cup sesame seeds, toasted slightly
4 tablespoons fresh lime juice
1 teaspoon soy sauce
1 teaspoon oil
1/2 teaspoon sugar
1/4 teaspoon salt
1 teaspoon minced onion
1/4 teaspoon curry powder
1/4 teaspoon fresh lime peel, grated
10 lime wedges

Cut chicken into 1 inch pieces. Combine the
lime juice, oil, sugar, salt, onion, soy sauce,
curry powder, and lime peel in a bowl and
mix. Marinate chicken cubes and water
chestnut slices in this mixture for at least 2
hours in the refrigerator. Bring to room
temperature. Divide chicken cubes and
water chestnut slices into equal parts for
approximately 10 or 11 small skewers. Roll
chicken cubes once more in marinade, then
in the toasted sesame seeds, then thread
onto skewers with slice of water chestnut.
Grill or broil, about 6 to 8" from heat, for
approximately 6 minutes, turning once. Put
a lime wedge on each skewer then place on
a warm serving plate. Serves 4.

Gee Bow Gai
Paper-Wrapped Chicken

1 pound chicken breast, boned and cut into small pieces

Marinade:
3 tablespoons plum sauce, see page 176
1 tablespoon hoisin sauce, see page 176
2 tablespoons cooking oil
1/4 teaspoon sesame oil
1 teaspoon sherry wine
1 tablespoon soy sauce
1 teaspoon sugar
1 green onion, finely chopped
1 few sprigs of parsley, finely chopped

Parchment paper or foil squares, about 3" square

Combine the above ingredients and marinate chicken for 3 to 4 hours, or overnight. Remove chicken from marinade. Wrap 1 or 2 pieces of chicken in paper or foil squares, repeat with remaining pieces. Deep fry packets, a few at a time, for 5 minutes or place them on a cookie sheet and bake in a 400 degree oven for 10 to 15 minutes or until packets puff up. Makes 16 packets.

Ming Salad
Chinese Chicken Salad

4 chicken breasts, bones, approximately 1 pound

Marinate 1 hour in:
1/4 cup soy sauce
2 tablespoons sherry wine
1 clove garlic, smashed
1 small piece fresh ginger, smashed
1/8 teaspoon five-spice powder

Remove the chicken from marinade and stir-fry until golden brown and cooked through. Cool and shred into small pieces. Set aside.

1 small head lettuce, shredded
4 green onions, slivered
1 bunch Chinese parsley
1/2 cup water chestnuts, slivered, rinsed,
and drained
1/2 cup slivered celery
1/2 cup chopped roasted peanuts
1 tablespoon toasted sesame seeds
1/6 small package py mei fun, deep-fried
(reserve half for sprinkling on top of salad),
1/2 teaspoon five-spice powder
1/2 teaspoon salt
1/4 teaspoon pepper
1 to 2 tablespoons sesame oil

Just before serving, toss all ingredients
together with the shredded chicken. Arrange in a serving bowl and add reserved py
mei fun to top of salad.
Makes 6 to 8 servings.

Py Mei Fun
*Py mei fun is a wire-like, dry
vermicelli sold in 8 or 16 ounce
packages. It can be found in
Chinese stores. It is made from
rice flour and when deep-fried
has a light crispness. The oil
must be very hot, 400 degrees
at least, to deep-fry properly.
Test the oil by throwing in a
single strand of py mei fun. If
the oil is hot enough, it will
expand and come to the
surface. It's quite something
to see. Use the wire strainer
for deep-frying. Put in only a
small portion at a time, as it
will expand and rise to the
surface very quickly. Scoop it
out immediately and drain.
This can be done ahead of time,
but store it in a dry place or it
will soften.*

Lychee Salad

Canned Lychee
This is an exotic, white-meated fruit. It is excellent as an after dinner or lunch dessert, served chilled with slivered candied ginger or with toasted sesame seeds sprinkled on top.

Do not border salad with py mei fun until ready to serve. It's nice to sprinkle a little on top of the salad, too.

1 Chinese-style Roast Chicken, page 119, boned and cut into pieces
Lettuce, your choice, torn into pieces
1 small can mandarin oranges, chilled and drained
1 small can lychees, chilled and drained
1/2 can sub gum pickles
1/3 package py mei fun, approximately 4 to 5 ounces
1 tomato, cut into wedges
1 small green pepper, cut into chunks
Toasted sesame seeds
2 cups sweet and sour sauce, see recipe page 173

Arrange lettuce pieces on a serving plate. Arrange all the fruit and chicken meat on the lettuce. Pour sweet and sour sauce over salad and border with py mei fun. Sprinkle sesame seeds on top. Serve cold. Makes 6 to 8 servings.

Beef

All About Flank Steak

If you have two packages of flank steak in front of you, one of which is darker than the other, select the lighter-colored meat. Also select the flank steak that is thicker than the others — this has come from a better steer. Usually the lighter one is a better tasting meat and comes from a younger steer.

I usually specify flank steak for stir-frying because of the high yield of lean meat, there is hardly any fat on it. If cut properly it will be very tender. In a lot of Chinese cookbooks you will see round steak mentioned for stir-frying. Round steak is too tough for stir-frying. If you watch the supermarket ads you will sometimes see good specials on New York steaks. If you compare the special prices of these cuts with the regular cost of flank steak, they are quite reasonable so go ahead and use these fancier cuts. If you want to freeze the meat wrap it securely. Do not freeze for too long, as it will get freezer burn. When meat is thawed you will lose a certain amount of juice. When you cook with New York steak, remember that it is very tender — don't ruin a beautiful piece of meat by cooking it to death. Top sirloin is another nice cut of meat for stir-frying, but try to select one that is not too fatty.

Ginger Beef

1 pound of flank steak, sliced into thin strips across the grain
1/2 tablespoon soy sauce
1 clove garlic, minced
1/2 tablespoon oyster sauce
1 tablespoon sherry wine
1/4 teaspoon sugar
Salt to taste
2 tablespoons cooking oil
2 1/2 tablespoons cornstarch

It is important to add the seasonings to the meat before the oil is added. If the oil is combined with the seasoning, or put on the meat first, it coats the surface of the meat and the seasonings can not penetrate.

Combine flank steak, sugar, soy sauce, garlic, oyster sauce, sherry wine, and salt. Toss to coat. Then add 2 tablespoons of cooking oil to the meat mixture and mix well. Next add the cornstarch and mix well. Allow meat to marinate for 15 minutes.

5 tablespoons oil
1/2 teaspoon salt
1/4 cup fresh ginger, thinly sliced
2 tablespoons oyster sauce
1/2 cup of green onions, cut in 2" lengths
1/2 cup basic soup stock, see recipe
page 169
1/4 teaspoon sugar
1/2 tablespoon cornstarch mixed with
1/2 tablespoon water

Put 3 tablespoons of the oil into a frying pan
or wok, that has been placed over high heat.
When oil is hot, add the marinated meat,
spreading it evenly over the bottom of the
wok. Cook for 30 seconds, then stir meat
briskly; remove to a bowl. Add remaining 2
tablespoons of oil to the wok, still over high
heat. When oil is hot, add sliced ginger and
salt, and stir-fry until you can smell the
fragrance of the the ginger cooking. Then
add the oyster sauce and swish around in
the hot oil. Add soup stock and sugar and
bring to a boil. Boil for 1/2 minute to bring
out the ginger taste. Then slowly stir in
cornstarch mixture until desired thickness is
reached. Add cooked beef and green
onions. Toss briskly. Serve immediately.
Serves 4 to 5.

*Remember, swishing the oyster
sauce into the hot oil adds that
extra fragrance and taste that
makes a great chef!*

Oyster Sauce Beef with Sugar Peas

1/2 pound flank steak, sliced thinly across the grain
1/2 teaspoon soy sauce
1 small clove garlic, minced
1 teaspoon sherry wine
1/8 teaspoon salt
1/8 teaspoon sugar
1 tablespoon oil
3 teaspoons cornstarch

Mix the soy sauce, garlic, sherry wine, salt, and sugar together, then add the flank steak. Add oil and stir. Add cornstarch and marinate mixture for at least 15 minutes.

5 tablespoons oil, divided
1/4 teaspoon salt
1 small clove garlic, smashed
1 small piece fresh ginger, smashed
1/2 pound fresh sugar peas
1/4 cup sliced water chestnuts, rinsed and drained
1/4 cup sliced bamboo shoots, rinsed and drained
2 tablespoons oyster sauce
1/3 cup basic soup stock, see recipe page 169
1/4 teaspoon sugar
2 teaspoons cornstarch, mixed with a little water
3 whole green onions, cut into 1 1/2" lengths

A Wok with Mary Pang

Put 2 tablespoons of the oil in a frying pan or wok that has been placed over high heat. When the oil is very hot, add marinated beef slices, spreading them evenly over the wok. Cook for 1/2 minute then stir meat briskly for 1/2 minute. Immediately remove meat to a dish. Place 1 1/2 tablespoons of oil into pan over high heat, and when hot, add salt, garlic and ginger, stirring until garlic and ginger are lightly browned. Then add sugar peas, water chestnuts, bamboo shoots, and sugar. Stir briskly then cover and cook for 1 minute. Remove vegetables from pan and add to dish with meat. Put the remaining oil into the hot wok. When hot, add oyster sauce and swish around. Immediately add soup stock and sugar, and heat until boiling. Gradually stir in cornstarch mixture until the desired thickness is reached. Add the cooked beef, vegetables and green onions then stir briskly. Serve immediately. Makes 3 to 4 servings.

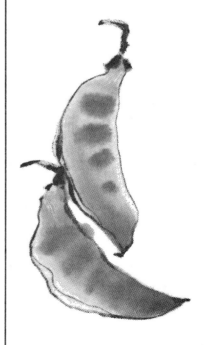

Stir-fried Beef with Tomato

3/4 pound lean beef, cut into 2 inch strips
for the marinade:
1 tablespoon soy sauce
2 tablespoons sherry wine
1/4 teaspoon salt, or to taste
1/8 teaspoon sugar
1 1/2 tablespoons oil
3 tablespoons cornstarch

2 tomatoes, peeled and cut into 8 or 10
wedges
1 green pepper, seeds removed and cut into
odd-sized chunks
1 small onion, cut into half and then into
slices
1 clove garlic, smashed and peeled
5 thin slices ginger, cut into thin strips
1/4 cup ketchup
1/2 tablespoon sugar
1/2 cup basic soup stock, see recipe page x
5 tablespoons oil
1 tablespoon oil mixed with 1 tablespoon
cold water
4 green onions, cut into 1 inch lengths

Mix together the flank steak, soy sauce,
sherry wine, salt, and sugar. Add the 1 1/2
tablespoon oil and mix. Add the 3 tablespoons cornstarch and mix.

Put 2 of the tablespoons of oil into a wok or frying pan that has been placed on high heat. Add the marinated beef and spread evenly over the bottom of the pan. Fry over high heat for 1 minute. Flip over like a pancake. Let fry for 1/2 minute. Stir briskly and remove to a dish.

Add another 1 1/2 tablespoons of oil to hot wok. Add salt and stir. Add garlic and brown. Add onions and stir-fry over 1/2 minute then add green pepper and continue to cook for another minute over high heat. Remove to a dish.

Add remaining 1 1/2 tablespoons oil to the hot pan then add ginger. Stir-fry until you notice the fragrance of the ginger. Take the pan of the heat momentarily to add the ketchup and sugar. Mix into hot oil. Return wok to heat and stir a few more seconds over high heat while it sizzles in the hot oil with the ginger. Add soup stock. Heat to boiling. Gradually stir in conrstarch mixture until desired thickness is reached. Lower heat to medium low. Add tomato wedges evenly over ketchup sauce. Flip over like a pancake after 1 minute. Continue to cook for 1/2 minute. Return stir-fried beef and vegetables to the wok and add green onions. Toss gently to heat through. Makes 3 to 4 servings.

If a curry taste is desired, add 2 tablespoons of top quality curry powder to hot oil at the same time as the ginger strips and stir into the hot oil.

Taking the wok off the heat momentarily while adding the ketchup prevents it from splattering all over when it hits the hot oil. It can be a mess to clean! And you lose a lot of the ketchup.

Green Pepper Chow Yuke
Pepper Steak

1/2 pound flank steak, sliced thinly across
the grain
2 teaspoons soy sauce
1 small clove garlic, minced
1 teaspoon sherry wine
1/8 teaspoon sugar
1 tablespoon oil

Mix together the soy sauce, garlic, sherry
wine, sugar, and steak. Add oil and mix.
Add cornstarch and mix. Marinate the meat
for 15 minutes.

3 tablespoons oil, divided
1/4 teaspoon salt
1 clove garlic, smashed
1 thin slice fresh ginger
2 or 3 medium green peppers, cut into
chunks
1 tablespoon oyster sauce
1/4 teaspoon sugar
1/2 cup basic soup stock, see recipe page
169
1 tablespoon cornstarch mixed with water
and 1/4 teaspoon soy sauce

Place 1 1/2 tablespoons of the oil in a frying
pan or wok that has been set over high heat.
When oil is very hot, spread the beef over
the bottom of the wok, fry for 1 minute to
brown. Then flip like a pancake and fry an
additional 1/2 minute over high heat.

Remove meat to a bowl. Add the remaining 1 1/2 tablespoons oil to the pan, again over high heat. Add the salt, garlic, and ginger and stir-fry until the garlic is lightly browned. Add cut green pepper, stirring briskly to coat pepper pieces with oil, cover pan and cook for about 2 minutes. Add the oyster sauce and sugar, mix. Add the soup stock and bring to a boil. Add cornstarch mixture and cook until thickened. Combine cooked beef slices with ingredients in the pan and mix briskly until hot. Makes 3 to 4 servings.

Chinese-Style Steak

2 16 ounce rib eye steaks
1/4 to 1/2 cup Basic Soy Sauce Seasoning,
see page 167
Salt and pepper to taste

Rub steaks on both sides with the basic soy
sauce seasoning. Marinate the meat for at
least 1 hour (longer if possible) before
cooking. Add salt and pepper to taste. Broil,
pan fry or cook on an outdoor barbecue.
Serves 2 to 4.

Cantonese Meat Balls

For Meatballs:
1 pound ground beef
1/2 tablespoons chopped green onions
1/4 small can sliced bamboo shoots, finely chopped
1 tablespoon sherry wine
1/2 teaspoon sesame oil
1/2 teaspoon salt, or to taste
1 egg, beaten
1/4 small can water chestnuts, finely chopped
1 tablespoon soy sauce

For cooking:
2 cups beef broth, or basic stock
6 tablespoons oil or fat for deep frying

Mix all ingredients thoroughly and shape into balls about the size of walnuts. Cook in boiling beef broth 3 to 4 minutes, or pan fry in a small amount of oil until brown, or deep fry at 350 degrees until brown. Makes 4 to 5 servings.

If you choose to cook the meat balls in broth be sure to use the left over stock for a soup recipe.

Mix deep-fried meatballs with your stir-fried vegetables and serve.

Serve with sweet and sour sauce as an entree.

Serve as appetizers with the following dips:
> *hot mustard*
> *sweet and sour sauce*
> *hot chili oil*

The Pork Recipes

Stir-fried Pork with Szechwan Preserved Vegetable

1 pound pork, sliced approximately 1/8"
thick, 1 1/4 " long and 1" wide
1/4 teaspoon salt, or to taste
1/4 teaspoon sugar
1 tablespoon soy sauce
3 tablespoons oil
2 1/2 tablespoons cornstarch
3 tablespoons sherry wine
1/2 cup Szechuan vegetable, sliced thin
(more if desired)
4 green onions, cut into 1 1/2" lengths

Add salt, sugar, and soy sauce to pork and
mix. Add 1 tablespoons of the oil and mix.
Add cornstarch and mix. Heat frying pan or
wok over high heat. Add the remaining 2
tablespoons of oil and heat until very hot.
Add pork, spreading it evenly over the
bottom of the pan. Cook over medium heat
until it browns. Flip it over like a pancake
and continue cooking until the other side is
slightly brown. Then stir-fry. Add Szechwan preserved vegetable and stir-fry. Total
cooking time is about 8 to 10 minutes, or
until pork is done. Swish sherry wine
sizzling down the hot sides of the wok.
Cover and cook 1/2 minute. Remove cover.
Add cut green onions and mix. Serve
immediately. Serves 2 to 3.

Szechuan preserved
vegetable
This is a vegetable that has
been preserved in salt and
pickled with chili powder. It
has an interesting, hot bite to
it. It comes in a can and may
be purchased at a Chinese
store. After opening the can
transfer the contents to a bottle
with a tight lid and refrigerate.
The vegetables come in big
chunks, simply cut off what
you need. You can steam it
with sliced meat, stir-fry it and
even put it in soups. Put it in
a soup recipe just long enough
to heat it through and to bring
out its hot flavor. Or eat it
sliced, cold. The chili powder
can be rinsed off, but leaving it
on gives it a much better hot
taste. It is quite salty.

Stir-fried Pork with Green Pepper

Lean pork steak is good for stir-frying. Save the bone for soup stock. Or when sliced from the bone, Boston pork butt is good, too.

3/4 pound pork, sliced 1/8" thick, 1 1/4" long, 1" wide
1/2 teaspoon salt, or to taste
1/4 teaspoon sugar
1 tablespoon soy sauce
3 tablespoons oil
2 tablespoons cornstarch
1 clove garlic, smashed and peeled
2 medium sized green peppers, stems and seeds removed, washed, and cut into odd-sized chunks
2 tablespoons sherry wine

Add salt, sugar, and soy sauce to pork and mix. Add 1 tablespoon of the oil and mix. Add cornstarch and mix. Heat frying pan or wok over high heat. Add remaining 2 tablespoons of oil and heat until very hot. Add garlic and brown. Add pork, spreading it evenly over the bottom of the pan. Cook over medium heat until brown on the bottom. Flip it over like a pancake and continue cooking until the other side is slightly brown, then stir-fry. Total cooking time is about 8 to 10 minutes, or until pork is done. All cut green peppers and stir-fry for about 1 minute. Then swish sherry wine sizzling down the hot sides of the wok. Cover and cook an additional 15 seconds. Serve immediately. Serves 2 to 3.

Curry Pork with Potatoes

2 pounds pork, cut into 1 1/4" cubes
2 tablespoons oil
Salt to taste
1 clove garlic, smashed and peeled
4 tablespoons curry powder, adjust to taste
3/4 pound potatoes, peeled and cut into 1" chunks
1 tablespoon soy sauce
1/2 teaspoon sugar
1 1/2 cups basic soup stock, see recipe page 169
1 1/2 tablespoons cornstarch mixed with 1/2 tablespoon cold water
4 green onions, cut into 1 1/2" lengths

Put oil into heated frying pan or wok and heat until hot. Add salt and stir. Add garlic and brown. Add curry powder and stir into the hot oil. Add pork, then soy sauce and sugar, stir-fry over high heat. Add soup stock. Bring to a boil then continue cooking over low heat for 10 minutes, then add potatoes. Continue simmering an additional 15 minutes, or until both the potatoes and pork are done. Slowly stir in cornstarch, mixing until thickened. Add green onions and mix. Serve hot immediately. Excellent with hot white rice. Serves 4.

If you can not eat pork for health or religious reasons, simply substitute beef or chicken for pork in any of these recipes.

A Chinese Barbecue Stove for Barbecue Pork and Spareribs

You may have noticed in Chinese restaurants how the barbecued pork is cooked in a special oven with gas at the bottom and the meat hanging in the center. Most people don't have such a stove at home! However, you can simulate one buy putting the meat on a wire rack in a pan that will catch the drippings. I have seen many recipes that say to put the meat in the bottom of the pan — don't do that. The drippings will collect around the meat and you will be simmering instead of roasting. You want the dry heat to circulate around the meat, as it does in a Chinese oven.

To prevent smoking you can put 1/2 cup of water in the pan. This will prevent the grease from burning and smoking when it hits the pan. It will also help keep the meat moist, yet you are not steaming it! It is important that the rack that meat is set on is a open wire rack, not a broiling pan. The air must be able to circulate around the meat.

I like to start the meat at a high temperature to sear it and seal in the juices. Then lower the heat to medium, 325 or 350 degrees, to continue the roasting.

To really baste the barbecued pork and ribs, it is best to remove them from the oven, closing the oven door, and then return them to the oven afterward. Figure out how much time they have been out of the oven for basting and add that back onto the cooking time.

Let the meat rest for about 15 or minutes after you have removed it from the oven. If you try to cut the meat right out of the oven it will fall apart. This resting period also allows the juices go back into the meat.

Selecting the Meat for Barbecued Pork

Chinese restaurants usually get a leg of pork, skin the fat off and render it for cooking; take the leg bone out and throw it in the soup pot; then cut the pork into strips for barbecued pork. The small pieces left over are used for stir-fry dishes. This is a little much for the home level. Many Chinese, for home cooking, buy the boneless Boston butt, which come from the shoulder. As a rule, most people prefer a less fatty cut, such as the boneless pork loin. Cut the loin into strips. Sometimes the grocery stores have good buys on the whole pork lion. Buy this and have the butcher (if you are on particularly good terms with him) debone it for you. When you look at a pork loin, the top part is a whole, large piece of meat — this is the part used for Canadian bacon and the one you can use for barbecued pork. The ribs that are left are referred to as back ribs, or as baby back ribs, which you can save to make the barbecued spare ribs. I have noticed that restaurants are charging a little more for these baby back ribs than for regular spareribs. If you save these back ribs from the whole pork loin, be sure you do not trim right against the bone, leave a little layer of meat on the ribs.

If you see pork loin on sale, take a look at it. Usually the big end of the pork loin will be less expensive than the smaller end because it contains a large bone, so you are not getting such a good deal after all. In addition, the smaller end has the baby back ribs attached, so you are getting two usable cuts.

Chinese-Style Barbecue Pork

4 - 8 ounce boneless pork loin strips (approximately 1" long, 1 1/2" wide, 1 1/4" thick)
1/2 cup sugar, adjust to your own taste
1 tablespoon salt
1 cup soy sauce
2 tablespoons sherry wine (optional)

The meat is being partly cured while marinating in the salt and sugar. This is what gives the pork that characteristic red color. If you prefer even more red you can add a little red food coloring to the soy sauce. Be careful, this coloring is very concentrated. You must add it to the soy sauce, if you try to rub it on the meat directly it will spot and your barbecued pork will look as though it has the measles!

Mix the sugar and salt together and coat pork strips. Let these stand at room temperature for at least 1 hour. (Letting it marinate overnight or a few hours at room temperature is best.) Add soy sauce and sherry wine to pork strips, coating well on all sides. After adding soy sauce and sherry wine, the minimum time to marinate is 45 minutes, but do not marinate overnight at this point or the meat will darken. It is best to use a Chinese soy sauce for this dish, as it is not as dark as the others. Turn pork strips at least once. Save some of the marinade, about 1/2 cup, and put it into a dish, adding 1 teaspoon oil. Use this to brush on all sides of the pork strips. Line a shallow pan with foil, this is so it will be easier to clean up. Place marinated pork strips, fat side up, on oiled wire rack in a shallow pan. Bake in the middle rack of a pre-heated 450 degrees oven for 15 minutes, turning pork strips once and brushing generously with sauce on each side. They should be quite brown at this point. Reduce temperature to 350 degrees and continue to bake, turning pork strips at least once, for 45 minutes, or until done. Brush the saved marinade on at least 2 times during cooking, once halfway through and again about 10 minutes before done. (Internal temperature should be 180 degrees on a meat thermometer). If you do not think it is brown enough, put it under the broiler for a minute, but watch it carefully, as there is a lot of sugar in this sauce and it will burn easily. Remove from oven, and let it rest of 15 to 30 minutes before slicing. Serve with a Chinese-style hot mustard, ketchup, and toasted sesame seeds.

Slice the pork into thin slices then fluff them up in your hands before plopping them on a plate. This will give the illusion of a generous helping of pork.

This is a very basic recipe that is good for learning the technique of cooking barbecued pork. If you prefer a spicier barbecued pork, such as you may have eaten in a Chinese restaurant, add five-spice seasoning or hoisin sauce. It does not take much of the five-spice seasoning, as it is quite strong — about 1/8 teaspoon added to the salt and sugar mixture is ample. If desired, you may brush on hoisin sauce that has been thinned with some of the marinade. This will give the pork a nice brown color. It is best to brush the hoisin on about 10 minutes before taking it out of the oven. For that beautiful high-glazed look, use honey thinned with a little water. Brush this mixture on the pork as soon as you remove the meat from the oven. Be sure to use a clean brush for this, not the one that you have been using for the marinade, as the original brush has touched the raw pork and could contaminate the honey glaze.

All About Spareribs

When selecting spareribs, buy those that are meatier, with very little bone showing. There are three types of spareribs catagorized by the weight of the ribs and the age of the hog; the light ones run 3 pounds or under per slab; the medium sized ones weigh 3 to 5 pounds per slab; and the heavier ones are those over 5 pounds per slab. This division refers to the entire slab of spareribs, from the smallest to the biggest rib, with the bottom piece (called the skirt) still attached. The 3 pounds and under are the most tender. The heavier spareribs costs less per pound than the lighter ones that come from the younger hog. If the ribs have been cut before they are packaged you will then have to ask the butcher if the ribs came from a heavier or lighter rib. You have probably noticed how tender the barbecued ribs are in a Chinese restaurant — this is because the chef often uses the lighter ribs and they do not parboil the ribs before cooking. The flavor is not boiled away!

You will notice that the rib part is much thinner than the skirt part (the lower part that runs the length of the ribs.) In order for it to cook properly, and be done at the same time as the rib part, make deep slashes at 2" to 3" intervals.

Chinese-Style Barbecued Spareribs

1 slab fresh young pork spareribs, 3 pounds
or less
barbecue sauce, see recipe page 170

Brush the barbecue sauce generously on
both sides of the spareribs and let stand for
at least 1 hour. Place marinated spareribs,
meat side up, on an oiled wire rack, which
has been set in a foil-lined shallow pan, and
bake at 450 degrees for 15 minutes. Reduce
the temperature to 350 degrees and continue
to bake for 1 hour. During baking, turn
spareribs and brush them with barbecue
sauce several times. The final basting should
be done 15 minutes before removing spareribs from the oven with the meat side up.
Do not be chintzy with the sauce! If it is not
brown enough, put it under the broiler, but
watch it carefully. Let the spareribs rest for
15 or 20 minutes. Cut them into pieces and
serve. Makes 4 servings.

*I use a good, natural bristle
paint brush with a unpainted
wooden handle as a pastry
brush. There is no reason to
pay exorbitant prices for a
"gourmet" brush. But be sure
to put your bristle brush away
in the drawer with your other
kitchen utensils when you are
finished with it or you may
end up finding it in someone's
paint kit.*

Nom Yee Spareribs with Peanuts

To cut spareribs into 1 1/4"
pieces
This requires a lot of work.
Have the butcher cut the slab
of spareribs into 1 1/4" strips
across the bones, the entire
length of the slab. (The
butcher can do this with an
electric saw.) Then at home
cut dead-center between the
bones to get the individual
1 1/4" pieces. If you cut
against the bone, the meat will
fall off the bone during
cooking. Save the shirt
(bottom part of the ribs) for
soup stock. If spareribs are not
available you can substitute 1
1/4" cubes of pork meat.

2 pounds fresh young spareribs, cut
into 1 1/2 inch pieces
2 tablespoons oil
Salt to taste
1 clove garlic, smashed
1 small slice fresh ginger root
1 tablespoon soy sauce
3 tablespoons nom yee (red bean cake, see
hint opposite page), mashed
1/2 teaspoon sugar
1 1/2 cup basic soup stock, see page 169
1 cup sliced celery
1/2 cup raw blanched peanuts, stir-fried in a
lightly greased frying pan until brown
1 1/2 tablespoons cornstarch mixed with 1
1/2 tablespoon water
3 green onions, cut into 1 1/2" lengths

Put 2 tablespoons oil into a frying pan or
wok that has been placed over high heat.
Add the garlic, ginger, and salt and stir until
ginger and garlic are brown. Add nom yee
and stir in hot oil mixture until it sizzles.
Add spareribs, soy sauce and sugar and stir-
fry over high heat until slightly brown. Add
basic soup stock, bring to a boil and cover.
Lower heat and continue to cook for approximately 25 minutes, stirring occasionally. Tilt the pot slightly and skim excess fat

off the surface. Add celery and peanuts during the last 5 minutes of cooking. Add cornstarch, stirring slowly until desired thickness is reached. Add green onions. Serve immediately. Makes 3 to 4 servings.

Nom Yee
Nom yee is a fermented bean curd that has been formed into small reddish cubes then packed in a brick-red sauce. It has a pungent flavor and smell and is usually used for slow-cooked dishes. It is quite salty. If the nom yee comes packed in a can, transfer contents to a glass container with a tight-fitting lid and store in the refrigerator.

Remember, adding the nom yee sauce to the hot oil and stirring imparts a much more fragrant taste than simply adding it with the soup stock.

If desired, slightly cooked potatoes, cut into 1" chunks, can be added along with the celery and peanuts. Add as many as you wish. I prefer red potatoes, as they have more body to them.

Sweet and Sour Pork with Sub Gum

Sub Gum

Sub gum are Chinese pickles that are available in cans in Chinese stores and some super markets. Buy the variety that is either whole or sliced, not the shredded type. Sub gum has a sweet yet tart taste. They can be chilled and eaten alone. The liquid in the can may be used in place of water in making the sweet and sour sauce, adding an interesting taste.

In preparing the breaded pork cubes for this recipe you can use the "double fry" method. Fry the pork ahead of time but only until it is slightly brown, but cooked through. Set aside until ready to use. Then, just before serving, fry the cubes a second time to re-crisp and brown them more.

Pour the hot sweet and sour sauce over the sub gum and pork cubes just before serving, so the pork will stay crisp.

1 pound pork, into 3/4 inch cubes
2 teaspoons soy sauce
1/4 teaspoon salt
1/8 teaspoon sugar
1 egg, beaten
1/2 cup flour
1/2 cup cornstarch
1 can sub gum (Chinese pickles)
Double recipe Sweet and Sour Sauce, page 173

Blend together the soy sauce, salt, sugar, and the beaten egg. Add the pork cubes to this mixture and marinate for 15 minutes. Remove meat and drain. Blend flour and cornstarch together in a paper or plastic bag and dredge marinated pork cubes in this mixture. Add 2 inches of oil to a frying pan or wok that has been placed over medium heat. Deep fry pork for 6 to 8 minutes until brown and cooked through. Remove pork from pan and drain. Arrange on a warm platter. Heat the sweet and sour sauce. Add the sub gum over hot pork cubes and pour the sweet and sour sauce over the dish. If you want a little extra color you can add pieces of tomato or green pepper on top as a garnish. Makes 4 servings.

Egg Foo Young

1/2 cup chopped pork, (fried in small
amount of oil, until golden brown)
1/2 cup coarsely chopped bean sprouts
1/4 cup coarsely chopped celery
1/4 cup coarsely chopped water chestnuts
1/2 teaspoon salt
1/4 teaspoon sugar
4 eggs, slightly beaten

1 to 1 1/2 inch oil in frying pan
1 recipe Chinese-style brown gravy,
page 172

Mix all the ingredients (except eggs) thoroughly, then gently mix in the eggs. Do not
mix the eggs too much or they will not bind
the other ingredients. Heat the oil to 350
degrees in a frying pan. Add one-fourth of
egg mixture, cooking on each side until
golden brown. Repeat 3 more times. Serve
the Chinese-style brown gravy over the egg
foo young patties. Makes 4 servings.

If you live next to a Chinese family and hear lots of pounding right before dinner, they could be remodeling, but chances are they are chopping meat. The Chinese, as a rule, chop their meat with a Chinese cleaver on a chopping board. I like to use two cleavers so that I can chop twice as fast.

Water Chestnut Tumble with Lettuce Cup

The pork, wrapped in lettuce leaves, makes for a very refreshing dish. Eat it like a taco or burrito.

Serve in a bowl that you have rimmed with lettuce leaves. Put a bed of shredded lettuce on the bottom of the serving dish to prop up the food.

This requires a lot of chopping work and is considered a special dish. Instead of pork, dry oysters that have been soaked and chopped are used to create a really special dish.

1 pound pork, chopped fine
1 1/2 tablespoons cooking oil
1/2 teaspoon salt
1 clove garlic, smashed
1 tablespoon soy sauce
1/2 tablespoon oyster sauce
1/4 teaspoon sugar
1 teaspoon sherry wine
Few drops sesame oil
1/2 cup water chestnuts, cut fine
1 tablespoon green onion, finely chopped
1/2 cup celery, onion, or any vegetable
1/4 cup mushrooms, finely chopped
1/2 cup basic soup stock, see page 169
1 tablespoon cornstarch, mixed with 1 tablespoon cold water
Lettuce leaves, large enough for a tablespoon of filling to be scooped on and the leaf folded over. You are to eat this with your fingers!

Add the oil to a frying pan and heat until hot. Next add salt and garlic and when garlic is lightly browned, add the pork. Stir-fry until golden brown, then add the soy sauce, oyster sauce, sugar, sherry wine, and sesame oil and mix thoroughly. Add the water chestnuts, green onions, celery, and mushrooms. Mix, cover, and cook for about 1 minute. Add the soup stock and when it boils, thicken it with the cornstarch mixture. Serve on a lettuce leaf.
Makes 4 to 6 servings.

Chapter Six
Sweets

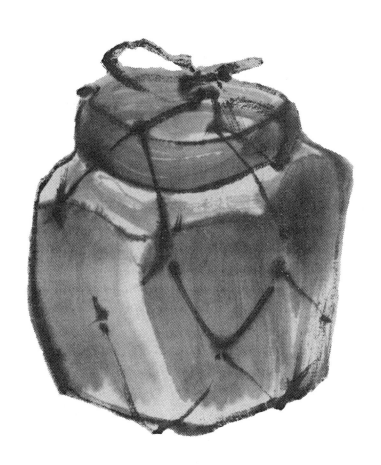

Sweet Recipes

Faht Go
Chinese Steamed Muffins

1 1/4 cup flour
1 1/4 cup Bisquick mix (packed)
1 cup sugar (if desired, brown sugar can be used instead of white sugar)
1 cup water
1 teaspoon vanilla

Mix together flour, bisquick, and sugar Gradually stir in water and vanilla. The mixture does not have to be really smooth. Fill muffin tins 2/3 full. Set tin in a steamer that has been filled with at least 1/4" of boiling water. Steam (as per steaming instructions on page 11), covered, over high heat for approximately 8 minutes, or until a toothpick comes out clean. If desired, sprinkle toasted sesame seeds on top just before removing from steamer. Makes 12 muffins.

This is a muffin traditionally served at Chinese New Year. When steamed properly the muffin will rise and pop open at the top, like a flower, into three or four petals. Popping properly means good luck!

Small muffin tins are nice for this.

The water can be colored with any shade of food coloring before being added to the dry ingredients.

All About Almond Cookies

When storing cookies in a tightly closed container, do not store with a moist-type cookie. This is because almond cookies, a crisp cookie, will pick up the moisture and become soft. Either store them by themselves or with other crisp cookies.

The Chinese traditionally use lard for their almond cookies. However, because people nowadays are very conscious of their cholesterol intake I have used vegetable shortening in this recipe in place of lard. Also, traditionally this recipe would be kneaded by hand. But, since so many families now have electric mixers I have specified using one with this recipe.

You can make sesame cookies using this recipe. After you have rolled the dough into a ball, press it into a dish of toasted sesame seed to flatten it and get the sesame seeds to stick. Place it on a cookie sheet with the sesame side facing upward. Do not use the egg wash as it is difficult to brush it over the sesame seeds.

You may have noticed at Chinese bakeries that the almond cookies are sometimes yellow or orange. The bakery has added food coloring to the dough. If you want to add food coloring, a few drops can be added to the eggs when they are beaten. Be sure to add the food coloring to a liquid, not the batter, or you will have funny yellow spots everywhere. Use coloring carefully, it is very concentrated.

This recipe will yield about 3 1/2 dozen cookies. If you are on a diet, and are limiting yourself to one cookie, then make it a big one. On the other hand, if you are making them for children, make them very small so they can have lots!

Almond Cookies

3/4 cup sugar
1 cup vegetable shortening
1 egg
1/2 teaspoon vanilla extract
1 1/2 teaspoons almond extract
2 1/4 cups sifted all purpose flour
1/2 teaspoon baking soda
1 teaspoon baking powder
1 egg yolk, slightly beaten, mixed with 1
teaspoon water
Small amount of blanched almonds

Cream sugar and shortening together. Add
the extracts and egg, beating well. Sift
together the dry ingredients and add them
to the creamed mixture, blending well.
Hand form dough into small round balls
about the size of a walnut, or smaller. Press
a small blanched almond or 1/2 of a larger
almond, into the center of each ball. Press
down and flatten ball of dough slightly.
Brush with egg yolk mixture then place on a
greased cookie sheet (not too close together).
Bake in a preheated 375 degree oven for 12
to 15 minutes, or until lightly browned.
Cool thoroughly before storing. Yield 3 1/3
dozen.

The egg wash is what gives the cookie that nice crackly effect.

Steamed Chinese Sponge Cake

This is a quick dessert to whip up when company comes unexpectedly.

This Chinese sponge cake is not sliced like regular cake. Put the blade of the knife or cleaver against top of the cake and press downward, through the cake. Otherwise, if cut in the regular sawing fashion, the cake will break into shreds and chunks.

Excellent as a shortcake for strawberries.

This is quite something to see; a sponge cake that is steamed instead of baked! It can be freshened up after a few days by putting it back in the steamer for a few minutes. You would think that it was baked fresh.

4 eggs
3/4 cup sugar
1 cup cake flour, sifted
1/2 teaspoon vanilla extract
1/4 teaspoon baking powder

Beat eggs for 10 minutes at high speed with an electric mixer, then blend in the sugar. Sift the baking powder with the flour and add to egg mixture at low speed. Line the bottom of a deep cake pan with wax paper and add batter. Steam for 15 minutes over high heat in a steamer, following the steaming instructions on page 11. Test with a toothpick to see if it's done. Insert the toothpick, if it comes out clean with no trace of stickiness, it's done. Remove from steamer. Before serving prop the cake pan upside down until cake cools.

Chapter Seven
Basic Recipes
and Sauces

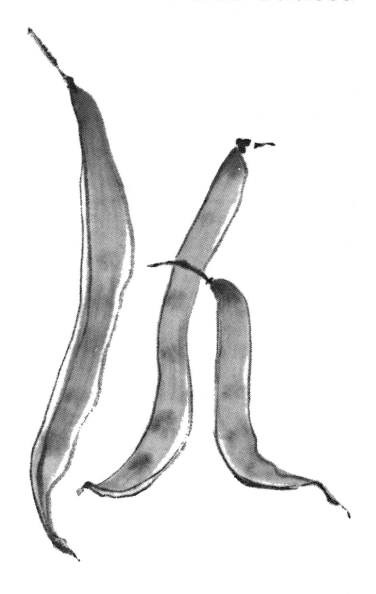

Basic Recipes & Sauces

Mary's All-Purpose Basic Soy Sauce Seasoning

1/2 cup soy sauce
4 teaspoons sugar (adjust to taste)
1 clove garlic, minced
2 teaspoons sherry wine
3 thin slices fresh ginger minced

Mix all ingredients thoroughly.

This is an excellent sauce to use for marinating fish, poultry and any type of meat. This sauce is not as sweet as teriyaki sauce, but if you like it sweeter simply add more sugar. You can double, triple or even quadruple this recipe. It gets even better after some time in a tightly closed container in the refrigerator. It will keep for months refrigerated. Take out what you need from the master container as you go. If there is any marinate left in your bowl, after you have cooked the dish, do not return it to the master container as it has been contaminated and will not keep.

Basic Batter

This is an excellent batter for anything that requires a batter.

1 1/2 cups flour
1 1/4 tablespoon baking powder
1 1/3 teaspoon salt
3 tablespoons oil
1 cup cold water
2 teaspoons sugar

Mix together the flour, sugar, baking powder, and salt. Gradually stir in oil and mix thoroughly, then slowly add cold water. Mix the water in well, be sure all the dry ingredients are moistened, then cover the bowl and refrigerate overnight. The next day, when you bring it out, the lumps will have softened and it will be easier to mix it in. This is a very important technique. If you wait until the next day, when the lumps are soft, you will get a nice smooth batter. This overnight technique also makes for a crisper batter!

Basic Soup Stock

2 quarts water
1 cup sliced uncooked pork or pork bones,
chicken bones, wings, neck, etc.
Salt to taste (1/2 teaspoon)

Put all of the ingredients into a big pot that
has been set over high heat and bring to a
boil. Reduce heat to low and simmer gently
for 2, or more, hours. Skim scum and fat,
strain soup, cool and refrigerate until ready
to use.

*For more detailed instruction
with hints and techniques see
page 139 in the soup chapter.*

Chinese Barbecue Sauce
Harry's Own Special Recipe

Some brands of hoisin sauce are thicker than others. If the hoisin sauce you are using appears on the thin side then do not add the water.

Do not return used barbecue sauce back to the master container. It is better to take out a smaller amount first and more if needed. That way you won't waste it.

1 pound hoisin sauce, this comes in a can or bottle, see page 176
1 cup ketchup, use a good thick one
6 tablespoons salt
2 1/4 cups sugar
1 cup soy sauce
1/2 cup water
2 tablespoons sherry wine
1 clove garlic, minced
1/2 teaspoon minced fresh ginger

Mix the ingredients thoroughly. This thick sauce will keep indefinitely in a covered container in the refrigerator. It is excellent for brushing on meats, fish and poultry. It is great for anything that needs marinating.

Black Bean Sauce

1 1/2 tablespoons fermented black beans
(dow see), mashed
1 tablespoon cooking oil
1 small garlic, minced
1/2 teaspoon minced fresh ginger root
1 teaspoon soy sauce
1/8 teaspoon sugar
1 teaspoon sherry wine
1/4 teaspoon sesame oil

Rinse the black beans briefly, then drain.
Mash it with the garlic and ginger. Combine the other ingredients and mix well.

Dow see - black beans
These are small fermented
beans. There are generally
found in Chinese stores packed
in a plastic bag that is placed
inside a round paper container.
This has a rather strange
smell, so its best to transfer to
a tight glass container as soon
as you can.

Black beans are the seasoning
used in lobster sauce (a sauce
for lobster, not one that
contains lobster).

This is a popular sauce with
seafood and meats.

This recipe can be quadrupled,
or more, and kept in a tightly
closed glass container in the
refrigerator.

Chinese-Style Brown Gravy

1 cup basic soup stock, see recipe page 169
Salt to taste
1/8 teaspoon sugar
1 tablespoon cornstarch mixed with 1 tablespoon cold water and 1/2 teaspoon soy sauce

Heat the basic soup stock then thicken with the cornstarch mixture. Stir in soy sauce.

The soy sauce is for coloring the gravy. If it is not brown enough for your liking, add a little more. But, be careful not to add too much or the soy flavor will be over powering.

Sweet and Sour Sauce

1/2 cup sugar
1/2 cup water
1/2 cider vinegar
1 tablespoon cornstarch mixed with 1
tablespoon water per cup of liquid (for a
thin sauce) or
2 tablespoons cornstarch mixed with 2
tablespoons of water per cup of liquid (for a
medium sauce) or
3 tablespoons cornstarch mixed with 3
tablespoons of water per cup of liquid (for a
thick sauce)

This can be used with fried wonton or any recipe that calls for a dip.

Put sugar, water and cider vinegar into a
pan and bring to a boil. Slowly add a few
drops of red coloring into the boiling
mixture until the desired red color is
reached. Be careful when you are adding
the coloring, as it is very concentrated.
Before adding the cornstarch take the pot off
the stove and wait for it to stop boiling.
Then slowly stir in the cornstarch mixture
until the desired thickness is reached. It is
very important that you do not add the
cornstarch mixture while the sauce is
boiling. The cornstach will cook immediately when it hits the boiling sauce and
lumps will forn. After adding the cornstarch return the pan to the heat and bring it
back to a boil. Slowly boil it until desired
consistency is reached.

It is easier to add the coloring when it is in the liquid form rather than after you have thickened it with the corn-starch.

All About Oyster Sauce

Oyster sauce is made from oyster extract derived from oysters that have been simmered for a very long time. It is not fishy in taste and is a favorite sauce of the Chinese. If you order a dish in a Chinese restaurant that has oyster sauce it will cost more than some other dishes. I buy oyster sauce in the 16 ounce container, but you can buy it in 5 pound cans! Try to buy oyster sauce in a Chinese store and ask the sales clerk which brand is the most popular with their Chinese customers. Look at the list of ingredients on the label, quite often some companies add MSG. If you are not fond of MSG do not buy this one. The more expensive brands contain a higher percentage of oyster extract. The less expensive have less oyster extract with more water and starch added. If you buy the more expensive brand you do not need to use as much to get the oyster flavor as you would with the less costly bottle. Oyster sauce can be kept as room temperature. It can be used for flavoring many things, such as noodles, rice, chicken, fish or as a dip. When using oyster sauce remember that it has salt in it so adjust the salt in your recipe accordingly.

Chinese Hot Mustard
The Mystery Solved

Have you ever, while eating barbecued pork, taken a little bit too much of that wonderful, hot Chinese mustard? All of a sudden everything breaks loose, your insides are burning instantly, tears are rolling profusely out of your eyes, your nose is all of a sudden clear, and you are searching madly for a glass of water or cup of tea to put out that inferno inside of you.

To get the really hot, hot as in a Chinese restaurant buy good dry mustard powder, (the really good one comes in a yellow can). Do not buy one that has any fillers. Put as much powdered mustard as you you would like in a small bowl then add water to it, slowly mixing it into a paste, to the thickness you want. There are two important techniques involved in making Chinese mustard. The first is that you have to mix it for a long time and the other is that is must stand a long time, preferably overnight. The more you mix it, the hotter it gets, and the longer it stands the hotter it becomes. If you let it stand overnight, pour a small amount of oil on top of your mustard and water mixture, tilting the bowl around so that it coats the surface. This will prevent a crust from forming on top of the mustard. Let it stand overnight in the refrigerator.

Two Popular Bottled Sauces

Hoisin Sauce
Hoisin sauce ia a reddish-brown piquant, but sweet, sauce that is used as a dip and is excellent for cooking, marinades and as a barbecue sauce. If in a can, transfer contents to another covered container and refrigerate after opening.

Plum sauce
Plum sauce is a sweet but tart dark red sauce that is very popular as a dip, especially with roast duck. If in a can, transfer contents to another container and refrigerate.

Foo Yee

Foo Yee, also spelled Fook Yu or Furu, depending on the phonetic spelling, is a popular Chinese sauce used for seasoning. It comes in bottles and consists of creamy-white cubes of soft bean curd made from soy beans and fermented in alcohol. The liquid in the bottle can also be used. I pour a little down the sides of the hot wok just before a dish is ready. The bottle can either be left at room temperature or stored in the refrigerator.

We kiddingly call it Chinese Linburger cheese, but it is not really that strong-smelling. In Chinese homes, it is often used as a condiment for white rice by adding a pinch of sugar and a few drops of vegetable oil over 2 or 3 cubes.

For those who like hot seasonings, you can find Foo Yee with chili pepper.

Hot Chili Oil

Making it yourself is a lot cheaper than buying it. And, most important, you know what type of oil is used.

This hot chili oil can be used on anything, but it is very popular for seasoning noodles, won tons and as a dip.

Caution: Use rubber gloves when cutting the dried chilies. Some people find that their skin itches if they handle the chilies without gloves. Do not rub your eyes or face after touching chilies as it will sting! Wash your hands (if no gloves are available) and the kitchen shears thoroughly after cutting dried red chilies.

1 cup cooking oil
24 dried red chili, approximately 1 1/2 to 2" long

The small chilies from Thailand are supposedly the hottest, even hotter than the larger ones. A 3 to 4 ounce package can be purchased from a Chinese store or from some supermarkets.

Put on rubber gloves. With a pair of kitchen shears cut the red chilies into small pieces and put into a stainless steel bowl. Do not throw away the seeds as they definitely add to the hotness. In a saucepan or frying pan heat the cooking oil until very hot. Then remove from the heat and let cool for about 4 to 5 minutes. Pour the hot oil over the red chilies in the stainless steel bowl. This step is very important as the hot oil opens up the pores of the red chili pieces, enabling the hot flavor to emerge and mix into the oil.

Hot chili oil can be made ahead of time and stored in a covered glass jar when cooled. The chili pieces will eventually settle to the bottom. You can use the chili oil immediately but the longer you keep it the hotter it will get. Double, triple or quadruple the recipe if you are fond of hot chili oil. It will keep for months in a cool place. Stir it occasionally.

About the Artist

Reni Moriarity is a potter and sumi painter. She has studied with Fumiko Kimura, Michi Osaka and Betty Ling. Ms. Moriarity is an active member of the Puget Sound Sumi Artists. She has won many awards for her paintings, including the Wang Chi-Yaun Memorial Award and the Benihana Purchase Award, at the Annual Exhibit Sumi-e Society of America in Wash. D.C. Reni has had a one-woman show in Tacoma, Washington and is currently showing works at a gallery in Seattle. She lives in Longbranch, Washington with her husband and son and a multitude of animals.

About Sumi Painting

Sumi painting, or ink painting, is an ancient oriental art form that originated in China and Japan. The art pieces are created on very fragile leaves of rice paper with a brush and a black ink stick, which is ground by hand each time. Its aim is to depict freely the essence of the objects of everyday life in a vital way within the confines of these materials. Ordinary objects are expressed spontaneously by the darkness and brightness of the ink as it flows and is absorbed by the rice paper. The relationship of the white space with the dark ink is very important. The page design of this book reflects this play of light and dark. Fruits, vegetables and sealife are some of the most common subjects for sumi painting.

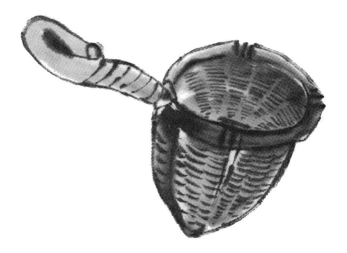

Index

ORDER FORM!

Give *A Wok with Mary Pang* to your friends so that they may enjoy a healthy stroll through Chinese cooking, too.

Send $12.95 + $2.00 ($4.00 for 2 or more books) postage/handling to:
Mary Pang's Food Products, Inc.
811 7th Avenue South
Seattle, WA 98134

Please send _____ copies to:
Name:_____
Address:_____
City_____ State_____ Zip_____

Please send _____ additional copies to:
Name:_____
Address:_____
City_____ State_____ Zip_____

We accept Visa, MasterCard, JBL, Diners, and Carte Blanche credit cards. Money orders and personal checks.

☐ Payment enclosed
☐ Credit card (circle one) :
Visa   MasterCard   JBL   Diners   Carte Blanche
Number:_____
Expiration date:_____